THE BISEXUAL OPTION
Second Edition
Fritz Klein, MD

SOME ADVANCE REVIEWS

"An outstanding contribution to our understanding of human sexuality. This updated edition of *The Bisexual Option* remains the most well-written and definitive book on the subject of bisexuality. Dr. Klein replaces mythology and ignorance with scientific insight and knowledge. This book has had and will continue to have a significant impact on our appreciation of the complexity of the wide range of human sexual expression."

Eli Coleman, PhD
Director and Associate Professor
Program in Human Sexuality
University of Minnesota Medical School

"Must reading for anyone seeking to understand the complexities and fluidity of bisexuality. Using a variety of perspectives (clinical, sociological, historical, and literary), Klein destroys the myths of nonexistence and neuroticism often attached to bisexuality. . . . Most important, the facts and findings disprove the false either–"gay"–or–"straight" labeling that has led to misleading research reports of sexual behavior and to widespread misunderstanding of bisexuality."

Amity Pierce Buxton, PhD
Author, *The Other Side of the Closet:*
The Coming-Out Crisis for Straight Spouses

The Bisexual Option
Second Edition

HAWORTH Gay and Lesbian Studies
John P. De Cecco, PhD
Editor in Chief

New, Recent, and Forthcoming Titles:

Gay Relationships edited by John De Cecco

Perverts by Official Order: The Campaign Against Homosexuals by the United States Navy by Lawrence R. Murphy

Bad Boys and Tough Tattoos: A Social History of the Tattoo with Gangs, Sailors, and Street-Corner Punks by Samuel M. Steward

Growing Up Gay in the South: Race, Gender, and Journeys of the Spirit by James T. Sears

Homosexuality and Sexuality: Dialogues of the Sexual Revolution, Volume I by Lawrence D. Mass

Homosexuality as Behavior and Identity: Dialogues of the Sexual Revolution, Volume II by Lawrence D. Mass

Sexuality and Eroticism Among Males in Moslem Societies edited by Arno Schmitt and Jehoeda Sofer

Understanding the Male Hustler by Samuel M. Steward

Men Who Beat the Men Who Love Them: Battered Gay Men and Domestic Violence by David Island and Patrick Letellier

The Golden Boy by James Melson

The Second Plague of Europe: AIDS Prevention and Sexual Transmission Among Men in Western Europe by Michael Pollak

Barrack Buddies and Soldier Lovers: Dialogues with Gay Young Men in the U.S. Military by Steven Zeeland

Male Prostitution by Donald J. West in association with Buz de Villiers

The Bisexual Option, Second Edition by Fritz Klein

The Bisexual Option
Second Edition

Fritz Klein, MD

Foreword by
Regina U. Reinhardt, PhD

The Harrington Park Press
An Imprint of The Haworth Press, Inc.
New York • London • Norwood (Australia)

Published by

Harrington Park Press, an imprint of The Haworth Press, Inc., 10 Alice Street, Binghamton, NY 13904-1580

Library of Congress Cataloging-in-Publication Data

Klein, Fred.
    The bisexual option / Fritz Klein.–2nd ed.
      p.   cm.
    Includes bibliographical references and index.
    ISBN 1-56023-033-9 (acid free paper).
    1. Bisexuality–United States. 2. Sex (Psychology) 3. Sex customs–United States. I. Title.
HQ74.K55 1993   92-44323
306.76'5–dc20   CIP

To M. S.

ABOUT THE AUTHOR

Fritz Klein, MD, is a psychiatrist in private practice, specializing in sexual orientation and relationship problems, short-term therapy using mainly neuro-linguistic programming and Ericksonian hypnosis, and HIV/AIDS therapy for gays, bisexuals, and drug addicts. He is coauthor of *Man, His Body, His Sex* (Doubleday & Co., 1978) and coeditor of *Bisexualities, Theory and Research* (The Haworth Press, 1986). Dr. Klein has lectured on human sexuality, given workshops on neuro-linguistic programming and hypnosis, and has been a visiting professor I.G.S./F.I.T., Florida. A board-certified psychiatrist, he is a member of the Examining Board of the American College of Sexology and the National Association of Neuro-Linguistic Programming.

CONTENTS

Both the heterosexual and the homosexual find the bisexual threat-ening. The myth of the bisexual's nonexistence and the stance of "either/or" is discussed.

The various dimensions, facets, and aspects of the bisexual's defi-nition are given. The Klein Sexual Orientation Grid is explained. An analysis of cultural and biological factors of sexual orientation.

The difference between emotional and sexual intimacy. The con-nection between intimacy and hetero- and homophobia. A profile of a heterosexual male who is able to be emotionally intimate with men.

An explanation of the Oedipus complex. The view that both homo-sexuals and bisexuals are able to resolve it successfully. An exam-ple showing how one bisexual male has resolved it.

Definition of neurosis and the various types of troubled bisexuals, as well as the healthy functioning of the bisexual.

Foreword

As a bisexual woman and a psychotherapist, it seemed both natural and important for me to research bisexual women because so little work had been done in this field, and of the little that had been researched, there were very few studies on women. When in the course of my work for a PhD, I found the first edition of Dr. Klein's book, it was immediately meaningful to me, both professionally and personally. Since that time, I have used *The Bisexual Option* as a tool for therapy in both individual and group work.

Fourteen years ago, when Dr. Fritz Klein first set out to write *The Bisexual Option*, neither the New York Public Library nor the *Index Medicus* contained any reference to literature on bisexuality. What little there was available largely denied the existence of the bisexual. Individual lifestyle preferences recognized today as "bisexual" were labeled "heterosexual with homosexual tendencies." Many treatments were used to assist in changing behavior, rather than supporting and maintaining a healthy lifestyle integrating all sexual preferences.

Dr. Klein's work presents a continuum of sexual, social, and emotional preferences over time, within which all of us can recognize ourselves and others around us. Self-awareness about one's sexuality is a continuing process, and *The Bisexual Option* is a book we can return to again and again for self-knowledge. I have found it useful myself to return to the book several times over the nine years I have been associated with Dr. Klein in San Diego.

In childhood, I erotically fantasized about and experimented with both boys and girls. My puberty was entirely void of feelings for girls, and these same-sex feelings did not return until my late teens, at which time they brought to me the recognition of my own bisexuality. I have spent my adult life happily married while maintaining secondary relationships with women with the full knowledge and consent of my husband.

Dr. Klein's presentation of the healthy bisexual and the troubled bisexual provides another scale on which we can locate ourselves. Identification on this scale as well changes with time and experience. The description of the healthy bisexual sets a model against which we can compare ourselves and toward which we can strive.

Many people are confused and fearful of recognizing and accepting their sexual preferences. Without direction and counsel they may never proceed beyond the question, "Am I a bisexual?" I recommend this book to my patients who are confused or uncertain about their sexual preferences. They return to therapy knowing they are not alone and with a clearer set of questions about themselves. Bisexuality is much more than a sexual preference. It is a framework of social, emotional, behavioral, and ideal preferences as well. We all have a need to belong, but the first acceptance we must have is our own.

While, as Dr. Klein points out, bisexuals have a high tolerance for ambiguity, they nonetheless represent the most complex state of sexual relatedness. In the end, it is not our preferences that lead us to a rich full life but rather our capacity for intimacy.

As leader, since 1984, of the Bisexual Forum, an organization founded by Dr. Klein, I have had the opportunity to work with individuals along the full spectrum of preferences so well described by the Klein Sexual Orientation Grid.

Meeting several times a month in a variety of group discussions and social settings, we have created in San Diego a social and support environment for a bisexual lifestyle. In the present state of awareness about bisexuality, the next stage of social development in America will appear when we are able to integrate a bisexual lifestyle into the prevalent social fabric, as has already occurred in many European countries. Dr. Klein's work has provided much of the foundation for this growth.

Regina U. Reinhardt, PhD

Acknowledgements

I am most grateful to the many people who have aided me in this work. First I want to thank all those who were kind enough to give of their time and share their histories with me. I have rearranged and changed the details of their stories to ensure confidentiality.

Chuck Mishaan, the director of the Bisexual Forum, was most helpful in every way. Both Aphrodite Clamar and Peter B. Field devoted many hours in diligent research. This effort is truly appreciated. I am indebted to Ed Hanlon for his enthusiasm and help. Special thanks go to John DeCecco whose encouragement made this second edition possible.

York, is the only one from Wilde to his wife that is known to have survived.)

From SEXUAL BEHAVIOR IN THE HUMAN FEMALE by Alfred C. Kinsey, Wardell B. Pomeroy, Clyde E. Martin, and Paul H. Gebhard, Copyright © 1953 by W. B. Saunders & Co., by permission of The Institute for Sex Research, Inc.

From SEXUAL BEHAVIOR IN THE HUMAN MALE by Alfred C. Kinsey, Wardell B. Pomeroy, and Clyde E. Martin, Copyright © 1948 by W. B. Saunders & Co., by permission of The Institute for Sex Research, Inc.

From SEXUAL DEVIANCE AND SEXUAL DEVIANTS edited by Eric Goode and Richard Troiden, Copyright © 1974 by E. Goode and R. Troiden, by permission of the publisher, Wm. Morrow & Co., Inc.

From TOWARD A RECOGNITION OF ANDROGYNY by Carolyn G. Heilbrun, Copyright © 1973 by C. G. Heilbrun, by permission of the publishers, Alfred A. Knopf, Inc.

From THE TWO WORLDS OF SOMERSET MAUGHAM by W. Menard, Copyright © 1965 by W. Menard, by permission of the publisher, Sherbourne Press.

From WOMEN IN LOVE by D. H. Lawrence, Copyright © 1920, 1922 by David Herbert Lawrence, renewed 1948, by Frieda Lawrence, by permission of The Viking Press.

PART I:
WHAT IS BISEXUALITY

Chapter 1

The Threat

The New York Public Library, known for its liberality, has two monographs on bisexuality. No books.

Why?

The *Index Medicus*, which lists all articles appearing in scientific journals on every conceivable medical subject, had 47 pieces on homosexuality. None at all on bisexuality. The category is omitted altogether.

Why?

The New York Psychoanalytic Institute, one of the major organizations of its kind in America and, indeed, in the world, has in its library catalogue over 600 items on the subject of homosexuality– and only 60 on bisexuality.

A few weeks prior to gathering the above information for the first edition of this book, I received a call from a friend asking me to lunch. Liz is the wife of a successful New York designer of women's clothes. There was an urgency in her tone that caused me to respond with an immediate yes, although I was quite busy.

"I'm free tomorrow," I said.

"I need to talk to you today."

"How about a drink around four?"

"Your office?"

"Fine."

When she arrived I poured her a drink. As we sat down she said, "Do you always offer your patients a drink?"

"I hardly consider you a patient."

"Well, I don't know. You'd better turn on the tape. I may never say again what I'm about to say now."

I switched on the machine.

"You know that Bill and I have been married for over twenty years."

"Quite happily, from all appearances."

"In our case appearances are not deceiving. We are very happy."

"So you and Bill are not the problem."

"In a sense, we are. How do I put this?" She sat a while staring into her glass. "About a month ago we were at a dinner party and this psychologist was there, an expert of some kind. He was holding forth on the nature of sexuality and he said that the homosexual and heterosexual were facts of life, and that the bisexual didn't exist. Bill challenged that opinion and the psychologist just took him apart, saying that the bisexual is nothing more than a closet gay. Bill really felt bad when we left. Bill said he didn't believe anything the psychologist said, but still he couldn't come up with an effective rebuttal. Since that incident we've been in constant dialogue over bisexuality. We've talked about little else, and it's begun to affect his work and our lives. There are the children to think about, and . . . oh my God, I don't know where to begin."

"Which of you is bisexual?"

"We both are." She stopped to light a cigarette. "Does that surprise you?"

"It's been rumored for years that Bill is gay and that your marriage is a front."

"Do you believe that?"

"No."

"What do you . . . what have you believed about us?"

"That you are a couple very much in love. That Bill is bisexual and that you are heterosexual."

"You didn't suspect about me?"

"No. I suppose because you haven't been that open about it. Bill has been known to flirt now and then with both men and women."

"He hates the 'gay' label. Not because of the connotation–God, half the people we know are gay–but because it simply isn't true. I feel . . . ah . . . well, that's it. I really don't know how to label myself. Neither does Bill. For years we entertained the possibility that we were superneurotic. But now Bill feels that he's not neurotic but just the opposite. Healthy."

"What do you think?"

"You know that there is a flood of opinion out there that would drown both Bill and me with an army of experts to say that you can't be bisexual and healthy. Bill is better off being thought of as gay, with his marriage as a front, than he is as a bisexual."

"Does Bill know you called me?"

"Yes. We both want to resolve this. We hate being told we don't exist sexually. Do we? Does the bisexual exist outside of being a confused gay, or just sex-mad?"

"Not according to many experts."

"How do *you* feel?"

"One, I think it's a presumption to tell people they do not exist. And two, I think the bisexual not only exists independently of the homosexual label, but exists period."

"Can you prove that?"

"Well," I laughed, "that's a tall order at the moment. I have a patient coming in a few minutes, but give me some time to think about it."

When Liz left I took down a book from my shelves called *Changing Homosexuality in the Male* by Dr. Lawrence J. Hatterer. I had read the book previously and I remembered that the point of view toward the bisexual was on the side of nonexistence.

In a list describing common and uncommon homosexual subcultures, Dr. Hatterer places the bisexual in the "disguised" group–along with closet queens and married males who regularly practice homosexuality. This almost universally held opinion is passed on to the public, both heterosexual and homosexual. And because it is easier to accept and understand the bisexual as a disguised homosexual, public acceptance of expert opinion goes for the most part unchallenged.

As disguised homosexual, the bisexual is by this process "reduced." We tend to categorize people, to put them into the most readily available group. In the worlds of commerce, government, and religion, this is to some degree logical. That this mistaken practice is also adopted by the individual in his or her search for self-identity–and held onto at all costs for lack of a suitable alternative–is tragic.

This is what Liz means when she says that Bill is better off being thought of as gay. Taking it further, if public and expert opinion are the only guiding standards to self-identity, Bill is "better off" *thinking of himself* as gay. Human beings need to belong. They need to communicate with their peer group. They need to sit around the communal fire not only in warmth but in dignity.

This is especially true in our society when it comes to the business world. In the world of business, banners of visible achievement are flown. Products are manufactured and sold, people are employed, money is made and lost, all in the name of business. Coca-Cola is as internationally known a symbol as the Union Jack or the Stars and Stripes. Buying and selling is most successfully carried on when the people flying the banners know the buyers to whom they are selling. Advertisers know that certain groups of people will remain loyal to a product for a lifetime–if that product can be correctly aimed by means of a direct emotional appeal to the given particular group.

In government, too, the virtue of loyalty can be extolled and exploited for all kinds of personal gain, both good and bad–all the more easily if the exploiters know their targets' place in society and can keep them there. Wars are "sold" this way, just as are worthier propositions, such as that all humans are created equal. As long as human beings can be simply classified as one thing or the other, the possibilities are endless.

It would be absurd to suggest that bisexuals are any more or less evil (or, for that matter, good) than heterosexuals or homosexuals. It is absurd as well to suggest that bisexuals are any more or less loyal than other groups around the communal fire. But the quality of loyalty may be different. What we have failed to see up to this point is that the bisexual may be less loyal to the status quo than to nature. Differences, freedom of choice, have been a threat to the group since before the beginning of recorded time.

One of the classic romantic questions asked of psychiatrists is, can one love two women or two men at the same time? My answer to that one is, "One can if one can."

Can human beings love both men and women at the same time? They can if they can.

What does this do to the individual's standards of loyalty? Is he or she able to carry the burdens of trust necessary in relationships that are more than transient or skin-deep? Or is he or she, by playing a dual role, a "spy"?

During wartime, spies, when captured, may be shot. An even worse fate may await citizens convicted of treason. They are often held up to particularly vicious public scorn before being killed. As much today as in the remote past, loyalty to "one's own" is held dear by the human race, north, south, east, and west. We simply do not condone spying or treason. They are acts so abhorrent that we are shocked by their existence, and often feel no guilt in erasing the spy, the traitor, so that no living trace remains. Being "drummed out" is, in a very real sense, being told that it would have been better had you never been born, and that from this time forward the position will be taken that you never were. "My country–right or wrong," is a line straight to the human heart, a place of worship in the human psyche.

The bisexual resembles the spy in that he or she moves psycho-sexually freely among men and among women. The bisexual also resembles the traitor in that he or she is in a position to know the secrets of both camps, and to play one against the other. The bisexual, in short, is seen as a dangerous person, not to be trusted, because his or her party loyalty, so to speak, is nonexistent. And if one lacks this sort of loyalty, one is so far outside the human sexual pale that one is virtually nonexistent.

Let us return again to Dr. Hatterer's interesting word "disguise."

A disguise is a deceit. A human being who spends his or her life in disguise is not to be trusted. It follows that a Jew in Nazi-ruled Europe who disguised him- or herself as a non-Jew to keep from being killed was not to be trusted by anyone. Yet, in retrospect, there are few of us with a claim to intelligence, let alone humanity, who would not trust the secret Jew above the S.S. officer who proudly showed his true face to the world.

In our society, with its strong negative view of homosexual behavior of any kind, it is quite understandable when bisexuals, or "closet" homosexuals, disguise their behavior. *But bisexuality is not disguised homosexuality, nor is it disguised heterosexuality.* It is another way of sexual expression. Although it contains elements of both heterosexual and homosexual behavior, it is a way of being, in and of itself, a way neither better nor worse than the more accepted ways of healthy heterosexuality and healthy homosexuality.

No matter what sexual orientation a person has, he or she lives on a continuum. Despite the certainty of eventual death, the life of an individual goes on until that time. During the course of a lifetime, each individual plays a number of roles: father, mother, soldier, teacher, heterosexual, homosexual, and so on. We take comfort in the labels; they help define our relationships with one another and with the world at large. Yet with each label we acquire, we limit our infinite possibilities, our uniqueness. It is our insistence on labels that creates the "either-or" syndrome. This is well illustrated by the mother and father who came to see me about the progress of their 25-year-old daughter, who was a patient of mine. They are a nice couple, prosperous, good churchgoing citizens. All their lives they have marched in a sometimes meandering, sometimes straight line for God and country. They have been rewarded with a comfortable life. When they came to see me everything was in its place except their daughter, who had recently announced to them that for the moment she was living with a woman. They were particularly upset because they were paying part of my bill for the therapy necessary after their daughter's recent divorce.

"Would you rather she hadn't told you?" I asked.

"What kind of a world is this where such a thing can happen?" the father replied.

"What has happened?"

"If this is where therapy leads, then to go on paying is throwing good money after bad." The mother was on the verge of tears. "A lesbian. We sent her to you and now she's a lesbian."

"Why do you say she's a lesbian?"

"She told us."

"She told you she was a lesbian? She said that?"

They looked at each other as though allied against some dark, sinister force. The mother answered. "She's living and doing God knows what with a *woman*. What else do you call it?"

"What did your daughter call it?"

"Whatever she calls it, she's too sick to know what it is." The father waved his hand in a gesture of dismissal.

"She says she loves this woman," the mother said, comforting her husband with a pat on the arm. "She actually wants us to meet her."

"How do you feel about that?"

"We don't know what to feel. Do you know that she and the woman she's living with have an open relationship?"

"What does that mean to you?" I asked.

"Well, it means that she sees other people as well. One of them is a man."

"She's had too much freedom. That's her problem." The father's voice was choked with anger. "A man here, a woman there. You can't live that way. You're one thing or you're another. That's the danger. Too much freedom. She's a lesbian now, no matter what she says to rationalize her disgusting behavior."

"Has she suggested to you that she's a bisexual?"

"We don't believe that for a minute," he said. "She's telling us that just so we won't make trouble for her."

"Why do you say that?" I asked.

"You're one thing or you're another." The father banged his fist on my desk. "I've lived long enough to know that, and I've been in business too long to believe anyone who says they're one thing today and another thing tomorrow. How long would you and I be in business, doctor, if we lived that way?"

"Your daughter's love life is not a business."

He got up, ready to leave. "One way or another, it's all business."

The calling-a-spade-a-spade point of view has a certain unvarnished, up-front honesty that I frankly admire. Artlessness is seldom without genuine charm, but that does not transform it into the truth. To understand the complexity of extradimensional choice requires more than mere straightforwardness, however tutored by experience it might be.

"Won't you sit for a while longer?" I pointed to his chair. "We all have your daughter's best interest at heart."

For the next half hour or so I became their ally in the wish for a psychosexually secure future for their child. It says much for them that after a few more sessions they did eventually come to accept, if not respect, their daughter's choice of love object. But they held fast to the view that "One way or another, it's all business."

Labeling is a tried and true method of eliminating the threats of uncertainty, ambiguity, fear. A familiar old myth illustrates this. In the form of an ill-contrived joke, it says that a man may father many beautiful children, be a transcendent lover of women, earn numerous degrees at the highest university level, discover a cure for an incurable disease, earn his country's most bespangled award on the field of battle; but should he fellate one penis, he will be forever known thereafter not as a loving parent, a lover, a scholar, a Nobel Prize-winner, a brave soldier, but as a "cocksucker."

There is another myth that, though not primarily sexual, is equally absurd in assigning a negative connotation, based on prejudice to begin with, to a mere fact of life. Many people in this country, especially in the South, consider a person with "one drop" of African-American blood to be "black." Why is this person not seen as white at least in degree? The answer is as simple as it is profane. A threat is best dealt with if it is dismissable. In the world of sexual choice the homosexual is the black. He is a "fag," a "fairy," a "cocksucker." We need not take him seriously. Somehow, God seems more secure in his heaven if we are not burdened with the element of degree, when we are judging threatening behavior, especially sexual behavior. Hence, if the bisexual is really a homosexual with a screw loose, his or her social and psychological obliteration is a comfort and a safeguard to all. This holds true for the homosexual as well as the heterosexual because existence, of however despised a kind, is preferable to, better than, a higher state than, nonexistence.

Abhorrent as "The Love that Dared not Speak its Name" has been to society over the centuries, at least no serious case has ever been made for its nonexistence; homosexuals or lesbians may have been despised for their "perversion," but their psychosexual existence has never been in question. The homosexual belongs. The lesbian belongs. He or she has a culture. He or she can be loyal to a team.

Our culture considers itself liberal and permissive, but the heterosexual view of the homosexual is, to say the least, negative. In a CBS poll, 72 percent of the people polled considered homosexuality an illness, 11 percent a crime, 9 percent a sin, and only 8 percent a preference. A Harris poll taken before perestroika and the breakup of the USSR found that 82 percent of males and 58 percent of females thought that homosexuals were the third most harmful group to the nation, behind Communists and atheists.

Is it any wonder that now, since the advent of Gay Lib and a measure of gay recognition, homosexuals may not want to recognize their possible bisexuality?

To most heterosexuals and homosexuals, the bisexual is an alien being whose dual sexuality opens up the possibility of their own sexual ambiguity. They cannot understand the bisexual's ability to share their own preferences but not their own aversions.

The heterosexual's erotic preferences and aversions usually do not permit an understanding of the homosexual. Homosexuals as well are baffled by attraction to the opposite sex. This creates two distinct camps from which banners can be flown. And though they may be ideological threats to each other, the two camps are as clearly distinct as, in the heyday of the cold war, the American eagle and the Russian bear. Their threat to each other is familiar, and the battle lines are clear-cut.

The wish to avoid conflict is natural and essential to life. Without peace of mind (if only of the kind available to the Sunday golfer), madness nips at our heels. Should we fail to defend ourselves, it will go for our throats. In our time, peace of any kind may be available only to the few who know themselves–and the many who keep their heads "securely" in the sand. Denial is one of the classic mechanisms by which this brand of security is sustained. For the heterosexual male, for example, the homosexual male's behavior may contain components of his own, but denial of the homosexual's label (and thence his role) is relatively easy. The heterosexual is not free to identify beyond certain vague, "neuter" acts, such as kissing or being fellated. But this same male confronted with a bisexual male must, if only unconsciously, deal with his own possible sexual ambiguity. The reason he is relieved to hear that the bisexual does not exist is that he thereby avoids his own inner conflict. If a homosexual male finds other males attractive, that fact has nothing to do with the heterosexual. But if a bisexual male finds both men *and women* attractive, that does have something to do with him in a way too close for comfort. The possibility of identification then is considerably broader. When the head in the sand comes up for air, what it sees may be unbearable.

Since, until now, bisexuality has been largely a negative, a *non-*state, a neither-nor–a disguised state of homosexuality or worse–how can it be described at all, let alone labeled healthy? Edna St. Vincent Millay notwithstanding, burning the candle at both ends–

despite its lovely light–has had a high price exacted upon it by both history and conventional wisdom.

The state of nonexistence is indeed dangerous. Liz and Bill, both children of their time, are among its victims.

The New York Public Library, the *Index Medicus*, and the New York Psychoanalytic Institute pronounce a harsh judgment on bisexuality by saying little or nothing. At least we now better understand why there is such a profound silence.

Chapter 2

Toward a Definition

What is bisexuality?

The prefix "bi" means two, or dual. We call a person with command of two languages bilingual. A simple enough definition. Bisexuality, however, is not so easily slotted. It is generally the most complex state of sexual relatedness with people. It exists to various degrees in everyone. Its dimensions are multiple.

Its prefix could even be called misleading: it is "bi" only insofar as there are two ends to the spectrum of sexual preference.

This very complexity breeds the wide range of misconceptions about bisexual behavior–as disguised homosexuality, transitional state from hetero- to homosexuality, and of course, the ultimate psychosexual dismissal, sickness.

Complexity in human behavior is fed by the exercise of choice. The more choices one's environment and inner state allow, the more complex the exercise; in the everyday life of the bisexual, for example, more intricate responses and signals are called for.

Although men and women share more in common than is normally perceived, they still are different in profound ways, and whether the bisexual is operating on a healthy or a neurotic level, these differences call for a wholeness of behavior, a dependence on the entire psychosexual spectrum, in their expression. At the office or the factory, for instance, the boss's or the partner's gender may matter to an employee as much as his or her ability. To succeed at work, to make it joyful or even tolerable, each employee must find ways of overcoming personal prejudice for the purpose of getting the job done. If, for instance, a woman says that she can work only with women, or a man claims that he is at his best only when employed with men, both face obvious obstacles to career advancement. The man or woman who can work equally well with members of either sex is operating in a more complex and adaptive mode than the man or woman who cannot.

Although sexual relations are work (if they are to have more than casual significance), they are also pleasurable and a kind of play. The combination of work and play with playmates of both sexes requires a subtlety of behavior, a suppleness in mind and body. For reasons that may be healthy or neurotic or both, bisexuals have a high tolerance for ambiguity and the resulting complexities. They may be at home in both worlds, strangers to none. Their range of physical/emotional responses is therefore made more complicated and demanding.

In *Sexual Behavior in the Human Male* Alfred Kinsey writes:

> The world is not to be divided into sheep and goats. Not all things are black nor all things white. It is a fundamental of taxonomy that nature rarely deals with discrete categories. Only the human mind invents categories and tries to force facts into separated pigeon-holes. The living world is a continuum in each and every one of its aspects. The sooner we learn this concerning human sexual behavior the sooner we shall reach a sound understanding of the realities of sex.

"Continuum" is the key word here. There are not discrete populations of heterosexuals, bisexuals, and homosexuals. With this in mind, it still is helpful to classify people according to experience and/or response. Kinsey developed a seven-point rating scale. The following is a figure of that scale together with his explanations.

FIGURE 1. Heterosexual-Homosexual Rating Scale

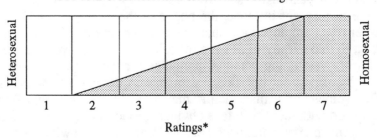

Ratings*

---

*Kinsey actually used the numbers 0 to 6 rather than the 1 to 7 which we use here.

FIGURE 1. Heterosexual-Homosexual Rating Scale

1. Exclusively heterosexual
2. Predominantly heterosexual, only incidentally homosexual
3. Predominantly heterosexual, but more than incidentally homosexual
4. Equally heterosexual and homosexual
5. Predominantly homosexual, but more than incidentally heterosexual
6. Predominantly homosexual, only incidentally heterosexual
7. Exclusively homosexual

Kinsey did not separate psychological reactions from overt experiences. There is of course a large difference between thought and action, between fantasy and experience.

Being identified by one's sexual orientation is relatively new in the history of humankind, going back only to the nineteenth century. Now, however, people act as if this classification of human sexuality is a fixed axiom in relationships between people.

Before we can adequately define "bisexuality" we first have to understand what sexual orientation is. When I started to study the concept of bisexuality, it became clear before very long that most people whom I interviewed were confused with respect to their sexual orientation. Their confusion lay not in what they thought or felt themselves but rather in the definition they could use for themselves and others. Many thought that they only had the option of two categories to describe their sexual orientation, namely, homosexuality and heterosexuality. Only a small percentage perceived the possibility of the third category of bisexuality.

It soon also became evident that no matter what definitions we gave to the three categories of sexual orientation, limiting it to only these three possibilities did not do justice to what these people knew about themselves and others. So I began to educate them to the Kinsey Scale and the notion of a seven-point heterosexual/homosexual continuum (see above).

In time, however, I found that even the Kinsey scale did not meet the needs of understanding what exactly sexual orientation means—too many questions were still left unanswered. If, for instance, we said a person was a 2 or 3 on the Kinsey scale, what did that mean exactly? The seven-point continuum did not satisfactorily answer the complexity of the concept of sexual orientation, the definition of which must take into account seven distinct variables:

A. Sexual Attraction
B. Sexual Behavior
C. Sexual Fantasies
D. Emotional Preference
E. Social Preference
F. Heterosexual ↔ Homosexual Lifestyle
G. Self-Identification

Sexual attraction is not synonymous with *sexual behavior*. A person can be attracted to one gender and yet have sex with the other. For example, Jane, a 34-year-old mother of two children, was monogamous in her marriage. She did not have sexual relations with women though she readily admitted to being attracted to females since early childhood.

Anna Freud has written that the sex of one's masturbatory fantasies is the ultimate criterion in homo- or heterosexual preference— an astute, even wise, observation on the face of it. But there are individuals who are capable of fantasy involving both sexes, of acting upon and being acted upon by both sexes, all the way to masturbatory orgasm. A bisexual interviewed in the preparation of this book told of a masturbatory fantasy in which he is hitchhiking and is picked up by an attractive couple who place him between them in the front seat. "We park somewhere in the woods, and they begin undressing themselves, at the same time kissing and fondling me. The woman is beautiful, with lovely breasts and shoulders, and he's very gentle but very masculine and he sucks me while the woman and I exchange passionate kisses. Later we get out of the car, and I fuck the woman and suck him off at the same time. We all come together. It's the best fantasy I've ever had. It always gets me off."

I asked him if he thinks of the man or of the woman during this fantasy. "I think of both. I mean I think of his cock and I think of her thighs and ass and cunt, and think of his coming while I'm coming in her. I think of them both. Everything."

Fantasizing both sexes at the same time is not the only type of bisexual imagery. Sometimes the fantasies are only of women, at other times men. *Sexual fantasies* is the third variable of sexual orientation. Over a period of time, changes occur, sometimes radically. Some people undergo a 3- or 4-degree change during the course of their adult lives.

The fourth variable, *emotional preference*, differentiates this aspect of sexual orientation from the previous three sexual variables. Some people prefer to have sex with one gender but are emotionally involved with the other.

The fifth variable of sexual orientation is *social preference*. To what degree does a person like to socialize with members of his or her own sex, and to what degree with the other sex?

Heterosexual ↔ homosexual lifestyle is the sixth variable. To what degree does a person live in the heterosexual social world? Does he or she have bisexual or homosexual friends, go to homosexual bars or clubs, and so on?

The last important factor is *self-identification*. Such identification influences many behavior and thought patterns. It was not until recently that people even had the option of thinking of bisexuality as a way of life–one had to be either a heterosexual or a homosexual. As we saw earlier with Bill and Liz, this can be a painful self-limitation. For example, a bisexual who views him or herself as a homosexual suffers not only because of the label. He or she may find nothing negative in being "gay." But one part of that person knows that the label is a lie, and suffers the anguish of anyone whose outward image conflicts with a personal truth that cannot be outwardly (and sometimes even inwardly) expressed.

Let me illustrate with the following example the difficulty of using the Kinsey scale in trying to decide where a particular man would fit on the seven-point scale, whereas by using the KSOG (Klein Sexual Orientation Grid–explained below) we can clearly delineate the man's sexual orientation. Kevin is a married man who dearly loves his wife and has sex with her on average once a week. However, about once a month he goes to the gay baths in his city to have sex with men.

With respect to the first variable of sexual attraction, Kevin rated himself a 6, that is, predominantly homosexual and only incidentally heterosexual.

If we use only Kevin's sexual behavior, we run into trouble with the Kinsey scale in that if we look at the number of his partners, Kevin should be classified as a 6 since he had sex with 12 men but only one woman. If, on the other hand, we look at the frequency of sexual outlets, he is clearly a 3 in that he had 52 sexual experiences with a female but only 12 with males. (For a definition of the numbers, see Figure 2, page 19.) In using the KSOG, we asked him to rate himself on this variable, sexual behavior. He answered that he is a 4.

With respect to the third variable, Kevin told us that during the past year his sexual fantasies were exclusively about men. This gives him a KSOG number 7 for this variable.

What about Kevin's emotional life? He only has one love in his life, namely his wife; he has never had any loving feelings toward men. Using the fourth variable, emotional preference, he is classified as a 1.

Kevin enjoys the social company of men and women equally. This places him as 4 on the grid.

Kevin lives almost exclusively among heterosexuals, and outside of the baths that he visits, he has as far as he knows no association with homosexual or bisexual people or organizations. For this variable, he is a 2.

Kevin labels himself a 5 on self-identification, the last of the seven variables.

Using the numbers of the Klein Sexual Orientation Grid, Kevin's profile is therefore: 6, 4, 7, 1, 4, 2, and 5. This example highlights the complexity of the concept of sexual orientation. Given this complexity, which one number would we assign to Kevin according to the Kinsey scale? How much more difficult still, then, to fit him into one of the three categories of heterosexual, bisexual, or homosexual. In my experience, however, I have heard arguments to support all three labels as the "true" or "real" category for any particular person.

Yet even these seven variables do not completely take into account the full complexity of sexual orientation. What we have left out of the definition so far is that over time many people change with respect to their sexual orientation. This is especially true for many bisexuals, gays, and lesbians. Where a person is today (in terms of behavior, feeling, and identification) is not necessarily

FIGURE 2. Klein Sexual Orientation Grid

VARIABLE	PAST	PRESENT	IDEAL
A. Sexual Attraction			
B. Sexual Behavior			
C. Sexual Fantasies			
D. Emotional Preference			
E. Social Preference			
F. Het/Homo. Lifestyle			
G. Self-Identification			

People rate themselves on a 7-point scale from 1 to 7 as follows:

For variables A to E.:

1. = Other sex only
2. = Other sex mostly
3. = Other sex somewhat more
4. = Both sexes equally
5. = Same sex somewhat more
6. = Same sex mostly
7. = Same sex only

For variables F. and G.:

1. = Hetero only
2. = Hetero mostly
3. = Hetero somewhat more
4. = Hetero/gay-Lesb. equally
5. = Gay-Lesb. somewhat more
6. = Gay-Lesb. mostly
7. = Gay-Lesb. only

where he or she was in the past or for that matter where he or she will be, or would like to be, in the future. The concept of an ongoing, dynamic process must be included if we are to understand a person's orientation.

Rather than use only one number to describe someone's sexual orientation, it becomes necessary to use a grid. The Klein Sexual Orientation Grid was therefore developed to take these factors into account (see Figure 2). This grid lets us see and understand at one glance what a particular person's orientation is.

The KSOG does have some limitations in that it does not cover some other aspects of sexual orientation: (a) it does not address the age of the partner; (b) love and friendship have not been differentiated in the emotional preference variable; (c) sexual attraction does not separate out lust and limerence; (d) the grid is unclear as to what is meant by frequency in sexual behavior–are we measuring number of partners of the number of sexual occurrences?; and (e) sex roles as well as masculine/feminine roles are not included.

Though the above dimensions of sexual orientation are not included in the KSOG, the seven variables and three time frames do cover its most important aspects. The grid is simple to fill out, and has elicited from many a person an "aha" reaction about their place in the sexual orientation continuum.

People differ infinitely–in height, intelligence, excitability, perseverance, color, age, point of view, nationality, religion, weight, sex, ability, and on and on and on. In every external and internal way they differ. There is no bisexual person who necessarily reflects a 50-50 degree ratio between his or her male and female preference. Such a claim would probably be as false as claims to fulfilling the ideal macho stereotype or the ultrafeminine type.

Within the continuum scale itself three different facets of bisexuality should be noted: transitional, historical, and sequential. A common view holds that all bisexuals are in a transitory stage–usually from heterosexuality to homosexuality. According to my findings and experience, this is true only for a small percentage of bisexuals. Bisexuality is used by such people as a bridge to change their sexual orientation from one end of the continuum to the other. Within their lifetimes, some people can and do change their orientation by more than one or two points on the Klein Sexual Orientation grid, but usually not in a short period of time. The change of emotions, ideals, and behavior necessary for such an alteration brings about, at times, the state of bisexuality. Often the bisexuality itself becomes the norm for that person, while a few people complete the swing to heterosexuality or homosexuality. For these few, this transitional bisexual period can be very short or can last for many years. It is also a two-way bridge–a person can travel the road from hetero- to homosexuality or from homo- to heterosexuality.

Historical bisexuality is demonstrated by the person who lives a predominantly hetero- or homosexual life but in whose history there are either bisexual experiences and/or fantasies. Sometimes the bisexual history is extensive, sometimes minimal.

Sequential bisexuality is quite common. Joan B., a patient of mine, began an affair with a woman after breaking up with her male lover. Two years later (when therapy commenced), she had just broken up with her female lover and shortly thereafter began a relationship once again with a man. In sequential bisexuality a person's sexual relationships are with only one gender at any given time. The frequency of gender change, of course, varies according to person and circumstance.

The total range of bisexual preference is extremely broad–from almost complete preference for one sex, to enjoying sex with either gender, to almost complete preference for the other sex. There is also episodic, temporary, experimental, or situational homo- or heterosexual activity. One example of episodic bisexual preference is the woman who sleeps with other women only when she is drunk. An example of temporary preference is the predominantly homosexual male who, when having an affair with a woman, prefers to have sex only with her. The experimental bisexual is represented by the person who switches the gender of his sex objects only once, say, to see what it is like. Many normally heterosexual men in prison practice situational bisexuality, given the circumstances. They would prefer females.

Public attitudes toward sexual preference also have profound effects on individual lives. "Coming out of the closet" has become the phrase most associated with newly avowed homosexuals, but it could apply to bisexuals as well. A "closet bisexual" practices in secret. The world at large does not suspect. (Chapter 8 discusses in detail the ways many bisexuals do manage to let their friends, associates, and family know about their sexual orientation.)

The subjective aspect of bisexual behavior must also be considered. A female prostitute who agrees to have a paid lesbian encounter might never consider herself to be bisexual. Male prostitutes who allow themselves to be fellated for money often do not consider this a homosexual act, or consider themselves bisexual.

A bisexual subculture would be yet another dimension of bisexual life, but if there is such a subculture it is too small to have any perceptible significance. With the increased media focus on bisexuality, however, we will probably see a new subculture develop, as bisexuals increase the frequency of their mutual interaction, and discover the extent to which they are a special group with beliefs and behavior different from those of other people.

Another aspect of bisexuality to be considered is the distinction between sexuality and intimacy. Sexual behavior and erotic feelings toward both sexes define the bisexual only, while intimacy is found in all kinds of human relations. We'll pursue this in much more detail in Chapter 3.

Finally, the most important thing to note is that the bisexual, the heterosexual, the homosexual each lives in a state of motion, and within that state anything in the psychosexual spectrum is possible. This of course makes all sexual labels (including "bisexual") a presumption, but a necessary presumption. These states of being can then be defined and located at certain points on the continuum.

Listen to two female bisexual patients of mine in a group session discuss where they both feel they are "at" in their sexual evolution.

Betty: "My trouble is I keep looking for the big neon-lights relationship–you know, the Handsome Prince who will carry me off to everlasting happiness ever after."

Wanda: "What if the Handsome Prince is a woman?"

Betty: "Well, I think about that too. The fact is I have more relationships with women than I do with men."

Wanda: "Sexual?"

Betty: "Yes."

Wanda: "What do you think of yourself? I mean, what do you think you are sexually?"

Betty: "Honestly?"

Wanda: "Of course."

Betty: "I think I've latched onto the bi title because then I can cover all the bases."

Wanda: "What do you really think?"

Betty: "Well, I live with this woman and I love her and I don't at the moment love anyone else so I think I'm moving out of the bi to the gay focus. My lover and I argue about this all the time. It's beginning to hurt our relationship."

Wanda: "She resents your fantasy of the Handsome Prince."

Betty: "No. Not at all. She keeps saying to me why don't I stop worrying about gay or bi and start thinking about us. She means, you know, concentrate on ourselves, what we are now."

Wanda: "It sounds like being bi is stunting you. I mean your conception of it. I'm bi, but in this group you're the one we all give the lesbian attention to despite the fact that, in action at least, I'm not bi but gay. I haven't had sex with or a fantasy about a man in years. You're the one we focus on, I think, because you keep trying to be one thing or the other. I think your Handsome Prince fantasy is just fine. Why not imagine yourself at some future point in another context. Hell, I'm mostly gay and I doubt if I'll ever sleep with a man for the rest of my life, but no matter what I say, I can't know that for sure. I think your lover is right. Why don't you stop worrying about gay or bi and think about you and her? If your lover can live with the Handsome Prince, you should be able to. She sees your possibilities clearer than you do."

A word about the biological, cultural, and psychological factors. Consider conception–the means, or, if you will, the miracle by which each new human life is begun: the egg and the sperm unite, a person is conceived. From this beginning, an embryo develops. It then becomes a fetus. Months pass and in time that a baby is formed, and when the months add up to nine the baby is born.

"Is it a boy?" "Is it a girl?" These are most often the first questions asked, in voices that suggest the gender of the infant has been determined by the birth itself. But it is in the sixth week after conception that the embryo begins to differentiate sexually. Until then, though genetically different, the "boy" and the "girl" look alike. During the sixth week the male gonads, the testes, begin to form. In the female the primitive gonad begins to develop in the form of ovaries as late as the twelfth week. The fetus is equipped with two complete sets of genital ducts–one male, one female. At some point during the third fetal month, one set of ducts proliferates while the other disappears, except for small remnants. Among all the various systems of the body, it is only the reproductive system that has two forms, or is, in a word, dimorphic.

It is the XY (male) or XX (female) chromosomes that program the sexual reproductive organs to develop into either testes (M) or ovaries (F). When the person is conceived, it is male or female only in the difference of its chromosomes.

So it *is* a boy, or it *is* a girl, as differentiated mainly by hormones and the male or female external and internal sex organs. Is that the end of the story? Does sexual identity and development freeze itself there in the moment of birth? No. In fact, the psychosexual development into male/female gender identity has not yet begun. It is post-natally that this boy or girl acquires self-identity. Gender identity is very much a function of biography—one's early life experiences, upbringing, cultural and social surroundings, and so forth. Together with its prenatal sexual program, this early imprinting is the basis of self-gender identity.

In 18 months, this gender identity has reached the point of no return. If, for instance, a mistake has been made and the baby is reared in the wrong sex, it is too late to change the rearing pattern because a new one simply will not take or, at best, will only partially take, and a confusion of gender identity is the inevitable result. If, however, the mistake is caught before 18 months, a sex reassignment can be instituted, and the boy or girl can be brought up in the tradition of the correct sex.

If an infant is brought up as one gender, he or she will develop that gender identity, even if it is the opposite of the infant's true chromosomal, gonadal, or hormonal sex.

Gender identity, however, has little to do with attraction for the opposite or the same sex. A man can have a strong, even super strong, male gender identity and still be attracted to his own sex exclusively. People do strengthen gender identity throughout their lives through sex with others, but the "feeling" of being a man or being a woman does not necessarily come from making love with the opposite or with the same sex. The renewal of strength comes from many sources in a person's environment, including intimate contact with a person, either male or female, whose own personal gender identity is nourished by the gender identity of the partner. A bisexual male, for example, having a deep relationship with a woman who lets him know in word and action that she loves the *man* he is, can in turn feel his inner maleness also with another man who is "turned on" by the same qualities the woman found exciting. What also should be put to rest is the idea that in homosexual activities there are male and female positions or acts, and that a specific position or behavior designates the person as playing the male or female role. A person's gender role, the outward manifestation of the gender identity, is not necessarily bound by what he/she does in bed. A gender identity can be reinforced by the attention received by a sex partner, but it is in no primary way dependent on it.

Gender identity, or how we see ourselves, is a cultural matter. Before that 18-month point of no return, any child can be programmed toward male or female self-identity, despite the child's true biological nature. There are cases of sexual assignment in children who have been genitally damaged. A case in point is offered by John Money and Anke A. Ehrhardt in *Man and Woman, Boy and Girl*.

> The extreme unusualness of this case of sex reassignment in infancy lies in the fact that the child was born a normal male and an identical twin, without genital malformation or sexual ambiguity. The idea of sex-reassignment would never have been entertained were it not for the surgical mishap at the age of seven months in which the penis was ablated flush with the abdominal wall. The mishap occurred when a circumcision was being performed by means of electrocautery. The electrical current was too powerful and burned the entire tissue of the penis which necrosed and sloughed off.

As Money and Ehrhardt point out, the parents of the child were young, rural people with grade-school educations. "They were understandably desperate to know what could be done. . . ." What they did, after much suffering and searching for answers, was consult a plastic surgeon familiar with the principles of sex reassignment, who recommended that the baby born a boy be reassigned as a girl. This was successfully accomplished through genital reconstruction. Hormonal replacement therapy with estrogen regulated feminization.

All of the external and internal medical application to this problem would have been pointless, however, if the parents had not brought the child up as a girl, with all that that culturally entails. We treat girls differently from boys, and how we do so has as much to do with their being boys or girls as their gender assignment at birth.

Is it a boy? Is it a girl? With what we now know about the imprint of culture on behavior, that question is no longer so easily or quickly answered.

The reproductive system, being dimorphic, treasures remnants of both male and female, and these remnants–to whatever degree–remain in every living person from birth to death. This is in its way germinal bisexuality, and although it can be programmed out of the conscious mind, it remains in the person, dormant perhaps but very much alive.

For both the heterosexual and the homosexual, the interpretation of dreams is the master key to possible truth. It is a well-known psychiatric fact that in dream interpretation the manifest content of a dream represents and is symbolic of unconscious ideas and objects. W. Stekel states that "every dream is bisexual," and in my own experience as well a very special facet of dream interpretation is constant–the heterosexual dreams from time to time of homosexual engagement, and the homosexual dreams of heterosexual engagement. "We can assert of many dreams," Freud wrote, "if they are carefully interpreted, that they are bisexual, since they unquestionably admit of an 'over interpretation' in which the dreamer's homosexual impulses are realized–impulses, that is, which are contrary to his normal activities." This is not to say (and Freud states this in the same paragraph) that all dreams can be interpreted this way, though many aspects of dreams are indeed sexual in nature. To interpret dreams, one must explore the dreamer's own associations to the dream's content.

A few years back a patient of mine, with a resolutely heterosexual manner and lifestyle, told me of a dream in which the thorn of a long-stemmed white rose pricked the palm of his hand. Although it had not been a nightmare, the dream woke him up, and he could not get back to sleep for the rest of the night. His revealing associations led us to a high school friend named Whitey with whom he had been close but not comfortable. From there the sexual nature of the thorn pricking his palm became evident. Another patient, proudly and exclusively homosexual, related a recurring dream in which he is performing fellatio on a wide-based penis with a small red glans. His associations not surprisingly led us to his mother's breasts.

In both of these cases, the men involved did not consciously want what their dreams represented. Those feelings and thoughts were in their unconscious.

If the human animal has bisexual components in its conscious or unconscious nature, what about the lower orders of animal life? Why are they less inclined toward bisexual behavior? They, unlike human beings, are stereotypically programmed to mate and reproduce without the creative elaborations allowed by the superior inventiveness of the human brain. Even very primitive societies use the variable possibilities in sexual relatedness to worship their God, or to strengthen their family and tribal life. In the Western world, male homosexuality was, until recently, seen as a negation of masculinity. Yet in some cultures male relations for the purpose of ingesting semen are esteemed activities. By the standards of the Kukukuku people of New Guinea, for example, such relations are an essential condition for growth into the complete man who is competent to survive as both tribal member and warrior. This practice of homosexuality is coupled with the practice and responsibility of heterosexuality, and helps keep the number of births in balance.

Another example of socially sanctioned bisexuality is provided by the Batak people of Lake Toba in northern Sumatra, who have an unchanging tradition of homosexual relationships between men and boys before marriage. Once married, however–and no man is permitted to remain in the single state–monogamy is the rule.

Being a man or a woman entails more than the ability to grow a beard or to menstruate. Studies of transsexualism and hermaphroditism show that a woman need not be genetically female in order to successfully mother in a female way an adopted child. The child will respond to what appears to be a woman if the human being behind the role believes herself to be a woman. She will succeed or fail as a mother not on her genetic reality but on the ability to give and to receive love.

Just as we have seen that male and female gender identity and its public expression, gender role, are set after birth, sexual orientation is also established postnatally. Whether one desires or actually has

sex with the opposite gender, the same gender, or both, is established during one's lifetime. But unlike gender identity, which is
fixed in early childhood, sexual orientation does in many cases
change later in life. The cultural factors of bisexuality, as well as
those for hetero- and homosexuality, are complex, and despite all
the hypotheses, our knowledge of all the causes of sexual orientation is still by no means complete. That cultural factors play the
dominant role seems beyond a reasonable doubt.

Chapter 3

"The Bisexual-Intimacy Level"

In our society fear of intimacy is expressed in part through heterophobia and homophobia–the fear of the opposite and/or the same sex. The main cause of the fear and resulting confusion is that sexuality and intimacy, though closely related, don't necessarily live together. They involve complementary but also strongly independent feelings and needs. Their compatibility is dependent on individual circumstance and social pressure.

Being close with a good friend who is laid up in the hospital, for example, can reach a level of pure, 100 percent intimacy without sex being part of it at all. But, if when the friend gets better and the possibility of sex arises, the intimacy becomes more complex. Or suppose two people share the oneness possible within an intimate situation to the point where a simple hug (whether born of sexual feeling, or merely affection, or both) is the obvious next step. If that hug is denied out of individual inhibition or social pressure, then the two people are less than 100 percent intimate, in that they are not responding freely to all the choices possible within the situation.

Sexual orientation obviously affects the nature of the sexuality. Everyone, however, has been oriented from childhood to think and behave sexually in a particular way; total intimacy is possible within that orientation, whatever it may be.

All persons, irrespective of where they are on the sexual orientation continuum, need what we call love. The wisest heads have pondered the nature of love, and no one has ever defined it to the satisfaction of everyone. What is life? What is love? No attempt will be made in these pages to answer such lofty questions. But we will attempt to answer a humbler question that relates to life and love: What is intimacy?

The crossing into the territory of intimacy is as natural–if less momentous–a crossing as the first vital breath taken on entering this world and the last patch of air breathed before leaving it. On the question of life or death we have no choice. Birth and death, no matter how gentle the passage, are the two great shocks of life. The first we view as generally positive, the second as generally negative. Before we were one with our mother; life begins with a kind of death–the traumatic termination of this unity. Intimacy, then, is strongly related to the experiences of birth and death. Since–in my view–we do not consciously remember birth, and don't return to this life to remember death, intimacy, the striving for unity with another human being, is our strongest link with the two most extraordinary events of our life. The feeling of liking or loving another person with complete trust, and the action of sharing emotions and experiences with that person, are seen and often described in relation to the two events. How often have we heard someone say, in the springtime of love, "I feel reborn"–or at the end of a relationship, "Part of me has died"? It's the great paradox. We welcome it. We fear it. We experience it to the degree that we welcome it. We deny it to the degree that we fear it.

The possibility, then, of a pure, 100 percent intimacy becomes a question of being willing to lose in order to win. What do I mean psychosexually when I say 100 percent intimacy? Imagine ten people, five men and five women, living in an isolated setting, sharing, liking, and loving in complete trust, but each exclusively with his or her opposite sex, or exclusively with his or her own sex. This could be said to represent 50 percent intimacy. If, on the other hand, each member of such a group were open to complete intimacy with both sexes, 100 percent intimacy would then at least be possible.

Motion is the condition, continuum the framework in which we can see and judge our capacity for intimacy. Within this framework, though, are three stages of intimacy–*minimal, circumscribed*, and *complete*. Every human being is born with the psychological potential and need for intimacy. A person's environment, neuroses, or both, can bring about an almost total inability to be intimate with other people; this reflects a *minimal* capacity for intimacy. *Circumscribed* intimacy goes beyond minimal but is eventually blocked because of an absence of complete trust in sharing experiences and emotions. "Trust" is the bridge word from circumscribed to complete intimacy. Once over this bridge a person is capable of selective *feelings* of liking and loving, and *actions* of sharing emotions and experiences completely with another person.

In addition to the degree of intimacy, the possible situations of intimacy are as varied as life itself. Still, we can divide intimacy into two broad types: sexual and emotional. The currency of sexual intimacy is physical satisfaction, sexual gratification. The closeness of the infant state is achieved once again but this time as a sexual adult. The need and desire for this type of intimacy is powerful, and its achievement usually starts at an early age and lasts into old age.

Emotional intimacy situations range from infant-mother, to child-parent, through social settings, to acquaintances and friends. Our earliest experience with intimacy is with our mothers–first in the womb and later as an infant. We're petted, rocked, embraced, fed, snuggled–our every wish fulfilled with mother love. Every human infant needs this experience to grow up capable of closeness and intimacy with other people. Next in the life of the child comes the intimacy of both parents and the family as a whole; separated from oneness with the mother, the child now shares in the emotional intimacy of the family. Until adulthood, ideally, the child loves and is loved by the family, and shares each member's experiences and emotions. He or she is, in other words, the beneficiary of complete emotional intimacy. The emotionally stunted adult was an emotionally traumatized child–the child who did not fully achieve total familial intimacy, whether as a result of having divorced parents or having a family unable to give and receive complete intimacy. The latter was the case with a patient of mine, an attractive, intelligent middle-aged woman who had never married, though she had had numerous relationships with men. She came to therapy because a man she loved very much wanted to at least live with, if not marry, her. She found the proposal terrifying. While she was growing up–on a farm in a small town in Pennsylvania–neither her parents nor her grandparents, who lived in the same house, had demonstrated emotion of any kind. "My parents slept in separate rooms, and I never saw them hug or even quarrel. When I was twelve I had my first period and I was afraid, but I couldn't go to my mother or my grandmother. And if it weren't for a teacher in school I wouldn't have known what was happening. My father was worse. Real American Gothic. We never said more than two words to each other and he never touched me. *Never*. When he died a few years ago my mother expressed no feeling at all, and when I asked her if she would miss him she said, 'Was meant to be, that's all.'"

Adults experience emotional intimacy every day in one degree or another. Three important social settings where intimacy is either expressed or implied are social gatherings, work, and play–for example in the form of sports. In social gatherings it's the chemistry of the people involved that allows for the sharing of emotions without fear. This sharing of sympathetic affections is at times so moving that even in social situations between strangers it can be meaningful. True, the very form, or formality, of some social situations–such as cocktail parties–makes meaningful intimacy with a stranger unlikely indeed. Yet it can and does happen. When it does we're not likely to forget it, even if we never see the other person or persons again.

At work, intimacy is the mortar of relatedness that builds the structure of accomplishment. Whether it is the pat on the shoulder for a job well done, the sharing of an agreeable lunch with a client, or your fellow employee helping you hold the cable in place, work situations often produce that quality of oneness between people that words can't describe. Many a job has been given up not because of the pay or the work itself but because emotional intimacy was lacking.

Think back to the emotional highs of sharing with your teammates an important victory or defeat on the playing field. Spectators, too, may share with others these emotional highs and lows. However, actual participation in sports allows for a closer intimacy because not only are emotions and experiences shared, but trust and usually friendship as well.

The worst punishment possible is isolation through the removal of intimacy. Solitary confinement is the worst punishment short of death. Emotional intimacy is a basic necessity for the social animal called "human."

A most important element of sexual and emotional intimacy is closeness through touching. Touching need not necessarily be sexual to be intimate. Feelings of love and trust transmitted by touch begin at birth, and this early contact is more complete than at any other time of life, except during the sexual act. But body contact occurs throughout life, even if in an adult's formal and ritualized fashion. The handshake of the stranger, the kiss on the cheek, the hug, the touching of the shoulder are some of the acceptable behaviors that all peoples and races possess. The specific form of touching may vary, but some form is universally necessary and desirable.

We can now understand somewhat better the causes of hetero- and homophobia. Essentially, they result from a fear of sexual intimacy following upon emotional intimacy. Emotional intimacy generally entails some form of body contact or at least proximity, and that, of course, can get too close for comfort. So to ensure that sex stays far enough away, we also sometimes avoid emotional intimacy. The heterophobic male homosexual is unable to imagine true emotional intimacy with a woman, wherein sexual intimacy is transcended and indeed, irrelevant. The progression to natural, affectionate physical contact is waylaid by his heterophobia. The homophobic heterosexual man is unable to imagine full emotional intimacy with a man, wherein touching and physical satisfaction on a nonerotic, nonsexual level are not only possible, but logical and necessary. His homophobia is stronger than his sense of the intimate truth of the situation.

Hetero- and homophobia also cause, in part, the formalization and ritualization of physical contact during intimate adult behavior. The full embrace is permitted only between lovers (where sexual intimacy is openly acknowledged), and sometimes between relatives (but not always, because of the underlying fear of incest). It's permitted between people in times of triumph and in sports where, for example, football players may hug because their "masculinity" is considered beyond question. It is also allowed after a disaster, or when in despair. At such times two men are permitted to hug, even kiss; taboos are forgotten and no sexual significance is attributed to the contact because it is regarded in the same light as the primary, "presexual" embrace of infancy.

What happens to someone who, over a long period, denies such a real and personal human need? What happens is neurosis–its severity will depend on how far-going the flight from complete intimacy is.

The substitution of pets for real human contact is one form of flight from intimacy. But certain kinds of human contact can themselves be substitutes. A former patient of mine could relate intimately only with children under the age of three or four. She felt safe in the expression of emotion with very small boys and girls because the chance of possible rejection was limited, and the burden of sexuality was–to her mind, at least–nonexistent. "I like to bite their little rumps," she once said, revealing a real need for intimacy, emotional and sexual, far greater than she was willing to see or admit to at the beginning of therapy.

Intimacy substitutes begin with the teddy bears and security blankets of childhood. Later substitutes may include the comfort of fur coats; contacts with hairdressers, masseurs, or tailors; or physical care called forth by real or pretended illness. All these are unhealthy only to the degree that they are utilized to the exclusion of people, but as Desmond Morris points out in *Intimate Behaviour*, "Any intimacy, however far removed it becomes from the real thing, is still better than the frightening loneliness of no intimacy at all."

The broader the possibilities for 100 percent intimacy, the wider the shadow of fear can become. Psychosexually, the fear monster of our time is like some two-headed dragon: the homophobia of heterosexuals and the heterophobia of homosexuals. The exclusivity of homosexual or heterosexual behavior splits us into two camps, separately helpless to slay this dragon–indeed, feeding him like some monstrous pet. We will slay the dragon only when we join together, yielding to what unites us (the capacity for intimacy) rather than to what separates us (fear).

When he arrives, our St. George may be a bisexual because he or she, having experienced sexual intimacy with both men and women, can show us that there is nothing to fear in selective emotional intimacy. He or she must be a *healthy* bisexual, with the capacity for emotional intimacy with both sexes. Without that capacity, possible in the healthy heterosexual *and* homosexual, there is only limited sexual intimacy, however pleasurable. And that is not enough, because constant sex without the element of intimacy adds up to the spiritual desolation inherent in promiscuity. This is not to say that selective random sex for its own sake is not good. But sex for its own sake is not enough for complete intimacy.

We can have it all. We can also have it even without complete bisexuality. Tom A., an acquaintance of mine, would not call himself bisexual, nor would his relatives, friends, or business associates label him so. He operates, however, at 100 percent intimacy through a loving marriage of 11 years and through the friendship of Paul W., with whom he has had an open-armed communion of feeling for nine years.

Tom has a good emotional and sexual exchange with his wife (their union has produced two children) and a good emotional bond with his best friend. Both Tom and Paul enjoy intimacy without sexual exchange occurring–an uneroticized intimacy. "Hell, what kind of question is that?" he replied, laughing, when I asked him if his relationship with his friend had ever reached the sexual stage. "Paul and I could fall into the sack together. Sure. But we don't need that. We have good times with our wives." He then related how once, on a fishing trip, Paul and he masturbated together at the end of the day. They had been away from home for five days and were sharing everything else. So why, they figured, should they go off in the bushes alone to masturbate? They felt close and hugged afterward before going to sleep. Tom feels that "You have to be close to another man to do that, so that you won't be judged–which is what everyone is afraid of." He says that if Paul and he ever "made it," it would be fine; though not necessary, it's also "no big deal."

On another occasion he said he would not be interested in having sex with another man since men don't turn him on. However, he doesn't mind closeness with men; in fact, he likes it. He thinks it's all the same, *if* one looks at people as people before looking at them as possible sex partners. Tom admitted, however, that he finds that hard to do with women, especially if "you see a really well-built woman–it's hard to see beyond that."

Tom is 34 years old, owns his own home in suburban Connecticut, and is a union electrician of good reputation and standing. He is an attractive, cheerful man whose capacity to give and take love enables him to be intimate with both sexes. He is lucky. He fell into the dragon's cave, and because he knew no fear, he came to no harm. I say he is lucky because the capacity for intimacy can have neurotic as well as healthy factors. Intimacy for Tom does not mean a show of power; nor is he a dependent type. We know that some people, for instance, marry for what they think is love, when in reality they harbor neurotic power/dependency needs having little to do with love. Intimacy on this level can be exploited for gain, with no giving. I call such intimacy "negative internal"—an absence of trust in liking, loving, and sharing with other people. But usually when I speak of intimacy, I'm speaking of something where the scales are reasonably well-balanced between giving and getting.

Tom, though not a bisexual, operates on a *nonerotic bisexual level* in that his capacity for emotional intimacy knows no gender limit. It is his own sense of freedom on this emotional level—as indicated by his self-rating of 4 (both sexes equally) on the KSOG for the Emotional Preference variable—that helps make Tom psychosexually healthy.

The healthy bisexual is healthy not because of his sexual intimacy with both sexes, but because of the enormous range of his emotional capacity. The healthy heterosexual and homosexual are also able to achieve emotional intimacy with men and women equally. The essential difference between the healthy bisexual, heterosexual, and homosexual is only evident in individual sexual preferences and behavior. Emotionally, the three groups all operate on a "bisexual" level, that is (as with Tom), they have no fear of emotional intimacy with either sex.

On the "bisexual-intimacy level," men and women are more alike than they are different, which of course isn't to say that no differences exist. For one thing, men and women treat intimacy itself differently. Important, too, is the role of culture in determining the manner of communication between men and women, between men, and between women, since the manner of communication affects the type of intimacy achieved.

The two types of interaction possible between two people are called *symmetrical* and *complementary.* In symmetrical interaction, the partners mirror each other's actions. It is based on equality and minimization of differences. An example would be two people of any sex, both excellent cooks, who try to outdo each other while preparing a good meal. Complementary interaction maximizes differences to the mutual satisfaction of both people. For example, if the husband makes the decisions and the wife follows them, he being assertive and she submissive, then complementary interaction is taking place. Both types of interaction are necessary for a prospering relationship, which needs both competitive behavior (symmetrical), and one-up and one-down behavior (complementary).

In relationships between men and women, our society stresses the complementary mode of behavior. Until recently little emphasis was placed on the competitive aspect of a male-female relationship. In fact, in many areas it was forbidden. In order for a man and woman to live successfully together, it was felt that they should only complement each other. This frequently meant that the woman buried her competitive drive in order not to run head-on into the man. Most people now realize that a good relationship requires that the woman also compete, in symmetry, with the man.

In friendship between men and men, and women and women, the intimacy type generally allowed is symmetrical. Little complementary interaction is permitted because that usually implies pairing, and pairing implies sexual intimacy. But since emotional and sexual intimacy are different, two male or two female friends might, if they chose, complement each other very well, with no implication of sexual intimacy necessary. The balance between the symmetrical/complementary types of interaction depends on the chemistry of the two people, male-female, male-male, or female-female. Competition, though, holds little sexual overtone. That is why many friends rely on it to achieve a satisfying intimacy level. But the "bisexual-intimacy level" allows for both, and it is in both that the transcendent closeness inherent in 100 percent emotional intimacy is achieved.

Chapter 4

Sexuality and the Oedipus Complex: A New Look

It is an early June morning. A man stands on a street corner on the Upper East Side of Manhattan waiting for the light to change. The sun is warm though not yet uncomfortably hot. The man is wearing a lightweight conservative business suit and carrying a briefcase. He might be a lawyer. Certainly he gives the impression of being a normal American male on his way to a normal American job. His normalcy is further attested to by his obvious pleasure in the women who pass by on every side. While he waits, he discreetly observes them, delighting in the fantasies offered by this pair of legs, that long hair, those breasts. The women take little notice of what the man is doing. It is, after all, normal male behavior. A few objects of his admiration smile, feeling safe in the gentleness of his style and the public context. He is observed by a policeman on the opposite side of the street. A taxi driver slows his cab, too, mistaking him for a possible fare. It would be safe to say that a dozen fellow citizens give him glancing attention before moving on. But had they seen the flirtation between him and another businessman as they both stepped off the curb, it is doubtful that a glance would have been enough. Confusion, and probably condemnation, would have followed, not because of the homosexual implications but because one of the men, seconds earlier, had been "girl watching" in a perfectly normal way.

One reason for the confusion is obvious. The theories of normal sexual development usually don't allow for a healthy bisexual. In order to broaden our base, let's take another look at the Oedipus myth, which is the cornerstone of the classical sexual development theory. Might we not, just possibly, be using it to shield ourselves from more truth than we have up to now been able to handle?

The Oedipus myth, as handed down from antiquity, goes like this: Oedipus is brought up by foster parents. While fleeing from Corinth to avoid the oracle's horrible prediction that he will kill his father and marry his mother, he kills an old man. On reaching Thebes he answers the Sphinx's riddle and is crowned king. Queen Jocasta is given to him as wife and they bear four children. The tragedy unfolds when Oedipus discovers that the old man he murdered was King Laius, his father, and that Jocasta, his wife, is in fact his mother. In revulsion and horror, he blinds himself. Jocasta commits suicide.

This myth supplied Freud with the paradigm for the Oedipus complex, a stage which every boy goes through at about the age of five in the course of normal development. The boy, who desires his mother, wants to kill his father, the rival for his mother's love. The power of these two forces–a death wish for the father, incestuous sexual desire for the mother–causes tremendous fear, which involves the loss of love of both parents in the form of retribution, castration, and even death.

To resolve this complex normally, the classic theory, first stated by Freud, holds that the boy must give up his mother as a sexual object. He does this by repressing his sexual wishes for her and transferring his desires onto other women as sexual objects. At the same time he represses his hostile wishes toward the father and instead identifies with him as a man. This is the normal resolution of the positive Oedipus complex.

In addition to the positive Oedipus complex, there is a negative Oedipus complex. In the negative Oedipus complex the boy wants to be loved by the father and to replace the mother as the sexual object choice of his father. This causes hostile feelings of rivalry toward his mother. And here, too, the boy's desires engender enormous fears involving the loss of love from both parents, fear of castration and death. Normal resolution calls again for the transfer of sexual desire onto other females and identification with the father (and not the mother). Its successful resolution depends on the innate relative strengths of masculine and feminine dispositions in the boy.

A girl also has a positive and negative Oedipus complex to resolve, but for her it's more complicated. She has to transfer her love from its original object, her mother, to her father. Then she must repress it and transfer it once again to other men, while identifying with mother.

The classical explanation of the Oedipus complex does not account for successful resolution by the homosexual and bisexual in a normal manner. The homosexual is supposedly fixated at a pre-oedipal level. Homosexuality is seen to derive from intimidation during infantile sexuality, which leads to the fear of the normal heterosexual object. Though admitting that the homosexual can function on an everyday level as well as the heterosexual, the orthodox classical view holds that any resolution except the "normal," heterosexual one is due to incomplete identification with one's own sex. The homosexual, then, is someone who combines the characteristics of both sexes and has not resolved the Oedipus complex successfully.

Freud wrote, "In all of us, throughout life the libido normally oscillates between male and female objects." And in 1922 Wilhelm Stekel, Freud's pupil and assistant, wrote that "All persons originally are bisexual in their predisposition. There is no exception to this rule. Normal persons show a distinct bisexual period up to the age of puberty. The heterosexual then represses his homosexuality. He also sublimates a portion of his homosexual cravings in friendship, nationalism, social endeavors, gatherings, etc. . . . If the heterosexuality is repressed, homosexuality comes to the forefront." In other words, few deny that bisexuality is found in the innate constitution of every human being; but for exactly the same reasons as given for the homosexual, the orthodox theory doesn't allow for a successful bisexual resolution of the Oedipus complex.

The classical view does not explain the healthy homosexual or the healthy bisexual, and is also murky in regard to women. The "straight" female finds some sanctuary in the theory, but there is *no* room in it for the homosexual or bisexual. I propose a new look at the Oedipus complex, as follows.

To resolve the positive or negative Oedipus complex successfully, the child must give up his or her sexual desires for both parents. The child must repress these wishes and substitute other people as sexual object choices. This transfer of the child's sexual wishes onto other people eliminates the fear of losing the parents' love, the fear of retribution by the rival parent, and the fear of castration and death.

Self-identification as male or female for the boy or girl has nothing to do with the Oedipus complex. The process of identification is carried on separately and begins long before the age at which the Oedipus complex begins. It starts with birth. The baby boy is treated differently from the baby girl, not only by the parents but by the whole environment. Different roles are required. By the time the child begins to speak, he or she already has a gender identity.

The healthy heterosexual has repressed his or her sexual wishes for both parents. But the heterosexual has to use more repression to resolve successfully the negative Oedipus complex than to resolve the positive Oedipus complex: for the former, the heterosexual must repress the sexual desire for one whole gender–his or her own sex. The boy cannot transfer his sexual wishes for his father onto other men, nor the girl hers for her mother onto other women. However, he or she is able to love someone of the same sex on an uneroticized level.

The healthy homosexual has also repressed his or her sexual wishes for both parents. But for the homosexual, more repression is necessary to resolve the positive Oedipus complex. The gender repression for the homosexual is for the opposite sex–the boy not being able to transfer his sexual love for his mother onto other women, nor the girl hers for her father onto other men. The homosexual, too, is able to express and feel love toward members of the opposite sex on an uneroticized level.

For the healthy bisexual male and the healthy bisexual female to resolve successfully the positive and negative Oedipus complex, it is necessary for them to repress their sexual desires for both parents. What is not repressed is the displacement of these desires onto others of both genders as sexual object choices.

The degree of repression for all three conditions–bisexuality, heterosexuality, and homosexuality–is environmentally induced. Abram Kardiner puts it this way:

> Every person is equipped with an inherent genital apparatus for sexual arousal and discharge, and from this standpoint the sexual drive may be considered inborn. But we cannot say because we do not know to what extent there is in man an inborn need either for a sexual object in general or for a sexual object of a particular gender. We do know, however, that the particular choice of object

that is made is markedly influenced by the growing child's dependent relationship with his parents. In this sense, the ultimate choice of object is a learned pattern of behavior.

Until recently ostracism for violation of the heterosexual standard through homosexual activity was the norm. The barriers have now been lowered somewhat. Gays and lesbians now march up Fifth Avenue on a Sunday afternoon just as the Irish, the Puerto Ricans, and the war veterans do. But more important, the American Psychiatric Association has removed homosexuality from its mental disease list (although the Association has kept listed as a disorder *any* sexual orientation if it causes persistent and marked distress).

The bisexual barrier, however, is still up. Both the heterosexual and homosexual view him or her as suspect, not a fully paid-up member but someone whose allegiance is with *the other* group. I find it ironic that this should be so. It is the bisexual who has repressed the least. He or she is able to react to both men and women on an erotic plane and to love members of both sexes on an emotional one as well.

The man who stood on the street corner is real. He is a stubborn fact, living under the same sun as you and I. He is not going to vanish. In the course of my life, I've met many bisexuals, both male and female. Some have been patients trying to improve their emotional relatedness to other people (as do some hetero- and homosexual patients), some have been friends, and some have been acquaintances. Paul is an acquaintance who became a friend, although we are not so close that I cannot describe him objectively. Paul's lack of repression in choosing partners of either sex has led him to a normal bisexual resolution of the Oedipus complex.

Paul is a handsome man in his mid-forties, about six feet in height, trim, clean shaven, with a dark intensity about the eyes. Although he is gentle, there is a kind of black Irish temper lurking behind his eyes, held in check by a keen intelligence. A first-generation American, he was only six months in his mother's womb when his father left home, eventually to wind up in jail. The year was 1932. The Depression was peaking, and his mother earned seven dollars a week as maid and cook to the Hamiltons, a wealthy Boston family. Paul was known for the next 19 years as "Nellie's boy."

Paul related his story in a series of taped interviews (four in all) over a three-week period. I asked him if he remembered much about his life between ages one and six.

"Yes. I'm blessed and cursed that way. I remember everything from two-and-a-half on. In the beginning my mother couldn't have me with her–she had to work–so she put me with a nice lower middle-class Irish family. I saw her only on Thursdays, her day off, and for years I had two mothers, the one who came every Thursday and 'Mom' Kelly, who was really a wonderful person. She had two teenage kids of her own, but I think she loved having a baby in the house. I called my mother 'Mother' and I called mom 'Mom,' and I loved them both very much but in different ways. What I mean is I loved Mom completely while I loved Mother the way you love someone who is loyal and you can trust. When I was about six, Mother made arrangements with the rich lady she worked for to have me stay with her each summer at the Cape."

"Did Mrs. Kelly have a husband?" I asked.

"Yes. I called him Dads, but I don't remember him at all except that he was quiet, gentle, and read the paper a lot. He must have been a good man because I never felt any bad vibes from him. He and Mom were very close, but honestly I don't remember him at all except I know he was there."

"Were any male figures important to you in your formative years?"

"Yes, there was one, but he served as a symbol more than a flesh-and-blood human being. But a powerful symbol. He was Mom Kelly's son from a previous marriage. He came to live with her for a time when I was about five and we became close. He must have been about twenty-five, maybe older, but not much. He owned a red roadster and he used to take me everywhere with him. Sometimes there would be a girl with him and I would ride in the middle. His name was Steven. He took me for my first haircut."

"Would you say you loved him?"

"I adored him. I don't know if I loved him but I adored him the way a boy adores a movie hero or a baseball player. I wanted to be like him. Then he went away. To New York. He became a singer on the radio and I used to listen to his program every week."

"Were you happy as a child?"

"Those first five, six years were really fine, and then, man, they sent me to school. No kindergarten, no nursery school, but right into the first grade. A Catholic school, nuns for teachers and, God, for the first time I came across really awful women. I mean, no one had ever hit me really hard until I went to school. I think they must have been a very sick bunch. I cried every day: I lived in fear of the strap and the ruler and I failed first grade.

"Summers became a haven away from school, and the Cape was beautiful except I was 'Nellie's boy' in a WASP environment. Mrs. Hamilton became a sort of closet mother to me, though. She had three children of her own, but she took me shopping with her. I liked her a lot. She was a terrific snob, but she took me to the public library for the first time, taught me music, and introduced me to a culture I never would have seen or felt otherwise. Now I loved her in another way. Very romantic. And she liked me too. But God, it hurt when there would be parties and picnics, and I couldn't go because I was the maid's son. I could play with the kids during the week, even wander into the living room, but when Mr. Hamilton came on weekends I had to stay in the servants' quarters or in the kitchen. I only saw him half a dozen times in seven years but, God, he loomed."

"Did you hate or dislike him?"

"I think I did hate him, yes. Hate is a strong word though. I more than disliked him. I never knew the man really. His children didn't like him. I think they hated him. He was that kind of Victorian gentleman who makes everyone uptight.

"So, anyway, I never knew where I stood at the Cape. Then after the second summer my mother planted me in a boarding school for boys. No warning, nothing. Suddenly that September I didn't go back to Mom Kelly but to this Catholic school, taught by Brothers this time, and they were worse than the nuns. I never saw Mom again. I pined for her for years. I nearly went crazy that first year. Mother admitted years later that she was afraid of losing me to Mom. That's why she did it.

"She was forty-one when I was born and, well, you can't blame her. I was all she had. She did her best for me considering the situation, but it hurt and I hated boarding school. The Brothers were brutal, and the kids were for the most part from broken homes and were pretty crazy. It was violent as hell. Sports, fights, constant bumping and shoving and hitting and hollering, endless conflict between the Brothers and the boys and between the boys themselves. Really awful. I was there for eight years. Christmas, Thanksgiving, and Easter I spent with Mother at the Hamilton house in Boston, and then summers on the Cape. I lived in two very different worlds at the same time. I didn't fit in at school because I wasn't really a lower-middle-class kid, and I didn't fit in at the Cape because I wasn't an upper-class kid."

"What were you?"

"A kind of hybrid, I think. I mean, I didn't want to be either. The kids on the Cape were more confused than the kids at boarding school. They had no love in them, though I think I liked them better as companions because at least you could get into the area of ideas once in a while. You see, I had no trouble with loving or being loved. I've always had a best friend or friends, and I've always had a woman in my life to love and be loved by. I did have friends at boarding school. Bobby O'Hearn was my best friend. I loved him a lot. Then I loved Joan, Mrs. Hamilton's daughter. We were the same age, and I had a crush on her from the age of nine to the age of fifteen. She cared for me as well, but I was 'Nellie's boy' and that was the big separation."

"Did you have sex with Joan?"

"*No*. No. I didn't have sex with anyone until I was twenty-two. I began masturbating at eleven, and I did it and did it and did it all through my teens into my early twenties."

"What did you fantasize when you masturbated?"

"Girls. Sometimes I used magazines, but mostly I just thought about girls. They were such a mystery to me. When I did finally have sex at twenty-two, it was perfect. Two weeks of constant lovemaking. I didn't tell her she was my first. I did later, though. She was very experienced and I was good with her. I remember before I entered her for the first time I said to myself just as I felt myself enter, 'I'm not going to be a priest.' It was good. It was really good."

"Had you dated in high school?"

"Oh sure. In high school and in the Air Force. I dropped out of high school and after then went into the service at nineteen. I would neck with girls. From fifteen to twenty-two, I would neck and masturbate. Not at the same time of course."

"Had you had any homosexual experience at all up to this point?"

"No, unless you count the time with this kid Bill when he and I were twelve. We were in a closet together hiding. Some kind of game, and I got an erection. I asked him to suck me off, although I don't think I put it in those words."

"Did he?"

"No. But I think he wanted to. I know I wanted him to."

"Did you continue having sex with women after twenty-two?"

"Oh yes. I met Nancy. I was working in the rare book field. Doing pretty well freelance. Mrs. Hamilton influenced me there. They had a magnificent library. Anyway, Nancy and I married. The baby girl came a year later."

"How was sex with Nancy?"

"It took about five years to get good and about ten to get really good. Now, after eighteen years, it's above high C. For the past five years every time we make love we come together. To me she's very sexy in a Gothic kind of way. And we love each other. She works at a private school. I work freelance. We've never had much money, but we live well and our daughter, seventeen now, is a nice person and a good friend to us as we are to her. We're happy, the three of us."

"Have you been 'faithful' to Nancy?"

"No. I've had four or five affairs–two major. One lasted four years. I loved the girl. She was different from Nancy. Big, warm, earthy. Sex was beyond description with her. I got myself into the Mother/Mom Kelly situation for four years and resolved a lot with it. Nancy knew about it. She has had affairs too. Not as heavy as mine, I don't think."

"Do you have an open marriage?"

"Not in the modern sense. We tell each other everything, Nancy and I–but we time it. I've never given to anyone, man or woman, the part of me that belongs to Nancy. Let's say you love someone, but they don't like ice cream and you do. Well, no problem. You find someone who does like ice cream, and you share it with that person instead of driving your mate crazy with accusations because she won't share *everything* with you. It's not possible to share *everything* with one person, but you can share the experience if you time it right."

"Have you had close male friendships in your life?"

"Yes. One lasted fourteen years. We loved each other as friends. Jim and I were as close as two people can get without being lovers. It was sexually a very straight relationship."

"When did you have your first sexual experience with a man?"

"I was thirty. Nancy was out of town one summer weekend with the baby, who was about five then. I was lonely, I guess. I took a walk around the city. This guy picked me up and we went to his apartment. Guys had been trying to pick me up for years but I had no interest."

"Why did you go with this man?"

"He was gentle and I liked his eyes. He had merry eyes and I suppose I was ready and just lonely enough. He had a nice place. Very tasteful. That helped. He gave me a drink. Two drinks. Then he said right out that he would like to go down on me. He did. It was so good, he was so good and loving at doing it that I stayed all night. He went down on me about six times."

"You remained passive?"

"Yes, except I responded. Really responded. Well, that was the beginning. I would call him once a week or so, and he would go down on me and we would sit around naked and talk. That was nice. I had never sat around relaxed and naked with a man before. And he told me things about my body that I had never heard from a woman. Like I had good legs. Now I do have good legs but women don't tell a man these things. I tell women if it's true. For instance, Nancy has a beautiful neck and a sexy ass and an absolutely perfect pussy. I tell her that. A lot. Just as I have told other women about how I feel about their bodies. This girl I loved for four years had a marvelous odor and great tits and I told her, but it never occurred to her to tell me, for instance, that I had a nice cock. If it weren't for men, I would never know I had a well-shaped cock. It's not important, but it is.

"For about three years, I went through a number of men who wanted to go down on me. Then I met a boy about twenty-two. He cruised me on the street. We went to his apartment and it evolved into a sixty-nine."

"Did you like it?"

"It took me a while, but now I like it a lot. Going down on a man you like physically or emotionally is very exciting. I can get very *into* it now."

"Have you ever loved a man?"

"Yes, I've loved Jim like a brother, friend, buddy, a lover with-out sex. Sexually, I came close once with this boy I met about a year ago. I felt something with him that I have only felt with a woman. I can't explain it, but in any case his job took him to Europe. If we had had more time, I think I could have loved him. I was never sure of his mind. I intend to fall in love with intelligent people, and to this day I'm not sure if he had as good a mind as he had a body. Also, men don't excite me as much as women do. Or I should say they don't excite me in the same way. I can become one with a woman if it's good between us. I have never been one with a man. It's hard to imagine, as a matter of fact. Sex with a woman is special to me. Sex with a man is wonderful, but somehow it's not special. Maybe because it's so easy to get, and I'm a man with a man's body and there's no mystery there. Women are very mysterious to me and I find that special. I'm happiest when I'm with a woman I love, just the two of us having a good time. But then again maybe I haven't met the right man. He would have to have a really good mind, a gentle way about him, and a nice body."

"What is a nice male body?"

"Trim, not too hairy–I'm hairy–and, well, I find myself very attracted to Oriental men. Though I've had good times with hairy men, so it really depends on the person. That's true of women as well."

"Do you think of yourself as bisexual?"

"Yes, but I don't advertise it."

I did not ask Paul why he does not "advertise it." I knew why. So do you. Although he might label himself a bisexual, others would condemn his behavior as neurotic. So he lives quietly, and from my observation after having met and spent time with his family, they and he are indeed happy people.

To the extent that the desire for members of one whole gender is not repressed, it is possible to erotically love both sexes. Little boys and girls learn what is expected of them early. Their traits and behavior patterns are reinforced as "male" and "female" not only by mothers and fathers but by the total environment. A successful resolution of the Oedipus complex does not include an identification with the parent of the same sex. That is a separate process.

Paul has, it would seem, successfully resolved his Oedipus complex by repressing sexual desires for his mother as well as male and female *parental* substitutes. As a bisexual he has not repressed his eroticism toward *men* or *women.*

This new look at the successful Oedipus complex resolution explains how not only the heterosexual male resolves it but also how women, bisexuals, and homosexuals do. It is simpler. It explains more. And more important, we now can understand the healthy heterosexual, homosexual, and bisexual much better.

Repression is necessary for a sane life. When a road sign says no left turn, we obey whether we want to or not, because our life or our neighbor's life depends on our choice. But surplus repression is not helpful or necessary. To continue not making that left turn when the sign has been taken down and the traffic pattern changed is to be a prisoner of habit.

Repressing incestuous desires toward the mother and father resolves the Oedipus complex successfully. The desire to be loved by both parents and to love them in return on an uneroticized level remains, enabling the person to displace his or her love onto others. Whether we end up healthy heterosexuals, healthy homosexuals, or healthy bisexuals depends on many factors. But the health involved depends on the successful resolution of the positive and negative Oedipus complex.

Paul's history shows one lifestyle of a healthy bisexual. Is heterophobia on the part of the homosexual and homophobia on the part of the heterosexual necessary? Is not the inability to achieve emotional intimacy with members of both sexes a crippling example of surplus repression? Does the possibility of intimacy, which might or might not lead to sexuality, need to be foresworn because we are hetero- and homophobic? Is not the ability to be emotionally intimate with both sexes a prerequisite for a richer, fuller life?

PART II:
BISEXUALITY AND HEALTH

Chapter 5

The Troubled Bisexual–
The Healthy Bisexual

In and of itself, bisexuality is neither good nor bad, black nor white, healthy nor neurotic. Bisexual individuals, however, can be located somewhere on the continuum between healthy and troubled, if not in terms of black and white.

When a subject (especially a sexual condition) that is new to the consciousness of a society or culture first begins to be discussed, either/or conclusions about the psychosexual validity of the subject are readily jumped to. One such conclusion is that the only state that is 100 percent pure is heterosexuality. Even if a disproportionate number of heterosexuals are found to be heterosexually neurotic, no stones are cast at the condition. The *condition* is not seen as the problem. The majority, so to speak, rules. In *some cases*, however, the heterosexual condition *is* the problem. But so entrenched in people's minds is the idea that the heterosexual way is the only virtuous way that its purity goes unchallenged, even in the most enlightened circles.

Homosexuals (including lesbians) and bisexuals, on the other hand, find that they must defend homosexuality and bisexuality *as such*; moreover, of the three groups, these two alone must defend their condition even at the highest level and the "best" particular examples that are manifested, let alone the "lowest" forms they take.

The highest level of any sexual orientation could be defined as those expressions of it that involve the greatest degrees of intimacy, from simple human concern to the complex love of two people in a long-term relationship. In saying this I don't mean to put sex for its own sake on a lower rung. When speaking of higher forms of sexual expression, the particular situation, circumstances, and people involved must all be taken into account.

To what degree is "bisexual neurosis" what the experts say it is? Before we can attempt to answer that, we must ask a more basic question: What is neurosis?

If there is one question above all others has been given no rest in the last half century, this is a strong contender. So with due apology I offer two points of view on it–one more or less generally held definition, and one from Dr. Karen Horney. The reader is invited to look into others.

According to Dr. Horney neurosis is a total personality distur- bance with its source in distorted parent-child relationships, and characterized by distortion in the individual's relationships with oth- ers and with the self, stemming from emotional conflicts and anxiety, and resulting in rigidity, suffering, impairment of functioning, and consequently a wide discrepancy between potential and achieve- ment.

A more general definition, given by Dr. Milton H. Miller in the *Comprehensive Textbook of Psychiatry*, edited by Freedman and Kaplan, is that neurosis is a syndrome characterized by psychologi- cal pain and anxiety, implying a kind of misadaptation that restricts the individual's overall judgment, his or her ability to make good contact with reality, and his or her capacity to relate effectively with others in the environment. Within this basic syndrome are a number of psychoneurotic reactions: anxiety neurosis, phobic neurosis, ob- sessive-compulsive neurosis, depressive neurosis, etc.

Many say that bisexuals generally do not have the capacity to fall in love with one person, that in fact the *majority* of bisexuals experi- ence only fondness, not love. I think this statement would make more sense if it began: "*Neurotic* or *troubled* bisexuals generally . . ."

Dr. Charles Socarides, a New York psychiatrist, makes, it seems to me, a similar omission: "They're [bisexuals] selling a phony sexual utopia in which the kingdom of the orgasm will supposedly replace the house of the ego." This statement, too, would make more sense if it began: "*Neurotic* bisexuals are selling . . ." Let's experiment for a minute with those opening words: "Neurotic ho- mosexuals are selling . . ." "Neurotic heterosexuals are selling . . ." It works in all three situations. Dr. Socarides is firing broadside at a large segment of the population on the basis of sexual preference. Does he mean to suggest that heterosexuals, since the onset of the sexual revolution, have *not* built altars to the orgasm at the expense of the ego? Or that homosexuals are not playing this losing game as well? To be honest, isn't a sizable proportion of the hetero-, homo-, and bisexual population, men and women, using sex in unfulfilling, destructive–neurotic–ways?

Dr. Natalie Shainess, a New York psychoanalyst, adds her bit of fabric to the patchwork of mythology about bisexuality: "The constant ricocheting from one sex to the other can create unstable friendships as well as a chaotic home life. If there are children involved this may confuse their sense of sexual identity."

Who would deny this? No reasonable person would deny that casual sex is sometimes indulged in at the expense of deep-seated love. But what these experts are commenting on is bisexuality in its *neurotic* and troubled condition. I would suggest only that their observations apply solely to troubled individual bisexuals–as well as hetero- and homosexuals–and not to the groups of people as a whole. Otherwise we regress back to the paranoid notions that all blacks are lazy, all Irish drunkards, all Poles stupid, all Italians gangsters, all Germans mass murderers, all WASPs unfeeling, all Jews economic conspirators, etc. It's too simple. It's too easy. It leads to dangerous mob-think.

To quote from Arthur Koestler in *The Act of Creation:* "The more mentally backwoodish a social group, juvenile or adult, the stricter its conception of the normal, and the readier it will ridicule any departure from it." We all have backwoods areas in our minds that feed, in darkness, on this evil. The groups most vulnerable to such brands of ridicule are those without the cultural rights to the concept of what is or is not "normal." The concept of normalcy is, in itself, only theoretical. As such, it is constantly changing, in much the manner of fashions in clothes. "Normal" is not a scientific, or mathematical equation, fixed for all time. "Normal" is only a set of values defined for the purpose of maintaining or securing economic, political, or other advantages for the society–or more likely, some *portion* of the society. When such values and the practices they may give rise to–the burning of witches, enslavement of Africans–become obsolete, they are changed or abandoned.

Margaret Mead had this to say about traditional attitudes in an article entitled "Bisexuality: What's It All About?":

Changing traditional attitudes toward homosexuality is in itself a mind-expanding experience for most people. But we shall not really succeed in discarding the straightjacket of our own cultural beliefs about sexual choice if we fail to come to terms with the well-documented, normal human capacity to love members of both sexes.

It is the *quality* of loving, not the gender of love's objects, that should come under fire. The quality of bisexual loving can be as high as the quality of heterosexual or homosexual loving. In our time the quality of all loving may be suspect, but it is not the responsibility of one group to carry the entire burden of neurotic behavior for a whole society.

Neurotic functioning is the evil genie who rides on the back of compulsive behavior. Sexual activity is one of the time-worn ways of getting the genie off our backs. But if the sex is compulsive, the genie does not go away; he sleeps, and because we no longer feel his hot breath on our necks, we experience the illusion of relief for a short while, until the genie wakes up to ride once again. The people most prone to this kind of behavior are the generally fearful, who must continually prove to themselves that they are not unlovable, unworthy, or otherwise unfit.

To act out a fantasy, both the props and the people involved need to be present. If you imagine an orgy of eating grapes fresh from the vine with your lover, all must be present and accounted for to make the dream come true. Because they live every day with the possibility of sexual intimacy with both genders, bisexuals, including troubled bisexuals, have more potential partners than do homo- and heterosexuals. For example: A heterosexual theatrical agent for showgirls has, if he is neurotic, more opportunity to blunt his senses with compulsive sexuality than, let's say, a heterosexual biology teacher in an all-boys school. The neurotic teacher would, if he could, but because he can't to the same extent as the agent, he enjoys a reputation for being safe and sane. The agent, on the other hand, enjoys a bad reputation, in spite of the fact that a healthy proportion of theatrical agents presumably are not hopping into and out of bed with their clients.

The bisexual, like the agent, has more opportunity for temptation. The healthy bisexual, like the healthy agent, uses his or her opportunities to pursue intimacy on *all* levels, allowing sexuality its place but not allowing it to become compulsive.

In *Neurosis and Human Growth*, Dr. Karen Horney makes the point that sexuality is frequently put to the service of neurotic needs because of the host of inhibitions and fears that fall into the bottomless pit of useless anxiety.

> . . . All of these factors may result in the neurotic patient's having sexual relations not because he wants them but because he should please his partner; because he must have a sign of being wanted or loved; because he must allay some anxiety; because he must prove his mastery and potency, etc. Sexual relations, in other words, are less determined by his real wishes and feelings than by the drive to satisfy some compulsive needs.

Flexibility would seem an uncontestably healthy quality, essential to the enjoyment of life's variety. Without it a person's outlook and inner world become increasingly narrow, to the ultimate extreme of disabling rigidity. But flexibility *without purpose* can pave the way to self-destruction. Dr. Horney continues:

> . . . Sexual activities become not only a release of sexual tensions but also of manifold nonsexual psychic tensions. They can be a vehicle to drain self-contempt (in masochistic activities) or a means to act out self-torment by sexual degrading or tormenting of others (sadistic practices). They form one of the most frequent ways of allaying anxiety. The individuals themselves are unaware of such connections. They may not even be aware of being under a particular tension, or of having anxiety, but merely experience a rising sexual excitement or desire. . . . A patient may for instance come closer to experiencing his self-hate, and suddenly there emerge plans or fantasies of sleeping with some girl. Or he may talk about some weakness in himself which he profoundly despises, and have sadistic fantasies of torturing somebody weaker than he is.

So, the uses to which opportunities and flexibility are put depend on the individual's psychic health, not on his or her sexuality. Self-hate is no more typical of one sexual-preference group than another. On the other hand, in any individual with preexisting troubles or neuroses, self-hate may grow–feed on itself–the more that it finds opportunities or outlets in compulsive behavior–much the same way someone with a history of heart trouble is more at risk from a diet of rich food and drink.

One problem that is peculiar to some troubled bisexuals is a lack of confidence in their gender identification. This is often the case with a man or woman who is not bisexual at all but homosexual, and afraid to let go of what is not actually an attraction to the opposite sex but rather an allegiance to an externally imposed idea usually rooted in the values of society. "I feel I can find my way back as long as I'm bisexual," one patient said to me. "Back to where?" I asked. "To the straight life," he answered. I then asked how he viewed the gay alternative. "Oh no," he insisted, "otherwise why would I be bisexual?"

Fears of intimacy and of being hurt drive people to seek safety in innumerable ways. For some people, bisexuality may be one of the more extreme suits of armor chosen for this purpose. Unconsciously reasoning that a moving target is harder to hit, they keep on the run, as it were, avoiding being pinned down to one sexual identity. But in attempting to circumvent the pain of loving and being loved, they more often fulfill their own worst fears.

The male bisexual may be quite healthy in his relationships with women but troubled in his sexual activity with men. Or he may have healthy relationships with men but be troubled in his dealings with women. And he can have troubles with both genders. In the first case he has the neurotic problems of the homosexual, in the second of the heterosexual, and in the third his neurotic sexual manifestations are peculiar to the bisexual. And the troubles aren't necessarily limited to sex. They can extend to all kinds of social, interpersonal contact.

Imagine a happily married man who also needs to express his sexuality with men. Imagine he is a successful businessman, living in a quiet, upper-middle-class town in, say, Connecticut, and working in a prestigious corner office of a Wall Street skyscraper. This man has a lot at stake in keeping up appearances. The pressure not to step out of line, not to embarrass his class, his town, his family and, most of all, the company, causes him deep anguish. No matter what solution this person finds to express his bisexual needs, socially induced guilt and shame will almost ensure his developing some neurotic functioning despite the fact that he may be quite healthy in other ways. In many such cases, the strain of maintaining a cover eventually catches up. The man is lost in problems imposed on him by elements beyond his control–unless he gives up what he's spent a lifetime building. This man is a troubled bisexual, because the world in which he seeks his identity is collectively opposed to the psychosexual "extreme" of his bisexuality.

Imagine a man or woman having difficulty with a spouse or lover of the opposite sex. Rather than face the difficulty, the person may resort to the typical troubled bisexual behavior pattern of running for comfort to someone of the same sex. This is a clear carry-over from childhood when, because one parent did not meet the child's real or imagined needs, he/she ran to the other parent. This bisexual runs from problems inherent in all relationships by periodically shutting the door on one sex and opening it on the other, shuttling back and forth in an endless, loveless game where no one wins, everyone loses.

In an article on homosexuality in *The New York Times*, Robert Gould distinguished two types of neurotic homosexuals.

> First, there are those who are disturbed and whose homosexuality reflects that disturbance symptomatically. An intense fear or hatred of the opposite sex would indeed constitute disorder, manifested in homosexual behavior.

He goes on to describe a second type of person for whom the neurosis is not related to the homosexuality itself. In this case the neurotic person also just happens to be homosexual. This distinction is equally useful in analyzing neurotic behavior patterns of the bisexual and heterosexual.

Yes, the troubled bisexual exists, and exhibits neuroses, but the healthy bisexual also exists, and flourishes, within his or her bisexuality.

Does the bisexual's ability to be intimate with both sexes raise more problems than it solves? Certainly a menu with many choices requires a more selective intelligence than one offering few. The necessity to discriminate no doubt confuses some people (as we've seen with the troubled bisexual), particularly at first. But loneliness is a great equalizer. Loneliness can be as democratic a condition as death. It respects no economic or class boundaries. Loneliness results from an absence of intimacy. The inability to be intimate is a condition that has grown over the centuries. Our preoccupation with material things intensifies it. Psychosexual health is best served by a flexible outlook on love and intimacy. Such flexibility relieves pressure on both the love objects chosen and on the chooser.

None of this is meant to be advocacy of sexual variety for its own sake. It is the knowing that it is there for the choosing, the awareness of and openness to sexual choice itself, that is liberating. Bisexuality itself may be less important than the possibility of it–the lack of *fear* of it. Intimacy doesn't require sexuality, sexuality does not require intimacy; but when brought together in combination they equal more than the sum of their parts. The healthy bisexual having the potential of sex combined with intimacy with both male and female has the possibility of enhanced sexual love.

It's true that some bisexuals play both ends against the middle in that they use people of both genders as sexual objects. To the extent they do, they're unhealthy and their bisexuality is unhealthy. At his or her best, the bisexual sees potential sexual partners first as human beings and then as sexual objects.

The bisexuals interviewed and studied for this book were all asked the question: "What are your feelings on your own bisexuality and bisexuality in general?" The answer was almost always the same: "Wholeness." Without exception healthy bisexuals (and some troubled bisexuals) speak of this feeling of wholeness, of feeling complete in the realization that the love of both men and women is there–if and when they need it. The difference between the healthy and the troubled bisexual can be measured by their degree of acceptance of this capacity as a responsibility as well as a need. The healthy bisexual uses freedom as a means for growth, for giving as well as getting intimacy.

Many bisexuals today are in danger of choosing heterosexuality or homosexuality merely because of the pressure put on them by our culture. Bisexuality is not considered a "normal" possibility by most orthodox psychiatrists. The pathological connotation that has been put on bisexuality for centuries has become dogma and has a near-holy place in the traditional psychiatric attitude. (Wilhelm Stekel, in a minority opinion, disagrees: ". . . Since no person overcomes completely his homosexual tendencies, everyone carries within himself the predisposition to neurosis. The stronger the repression, the stronger is also the neurotic reaction . . . In the case of the homosexual the repressed and incompletely conquered heterosexuality furnishes the disposition towards neurosis. . . . These generalizations already show that the healthy person must act as a bisexual being.")

The insecure person tends to reject, the mature person to accept. Sexual labels divide us into the known "we" and the feared "them." No matter which label or behavior pattern our own individual inclinations most closely conform to, we might at least entertain the notion of opening our minds and lives to people of all sexual orientations.

Chapter 6

The Troubled Bisexual–
Profiles

Because one person's neurosis may be another's saving grace, the question of who is, who is not, or who may be psychosexually troubled depends on where you stand. A good therapist tries to stand close enough to be of help yet far enough away to see the whole person. He or she also tries to take different points of view at different times in therapy sessions so that the sum of perspectives approaches something reasonably close to the truth of the matter.

The profiles in this chapter represent a sampling of what I feel are essentially troubled bisexuals with whom I have worked in this fashion–trying to merge objectivity with concern, and avoiding any fixed point of view that would reduce a living person to a mere snapshot.

Nora W.

Tall, with blue-black hair, large, warm brown eyes, and a smooth olive complexion, Nora is strikingly attractive.

"Let's begin with essential information," I suggested at our first meeting. "How old are you? Where were you born and where are you living now?"

"I'm thirty-four. I was born in Brooklyn. I still live in Brooklyn."

"Have you ever lived any place else?"

"No. Not really. Not for any great length of time. I was brought up in the Red Hook section. It's very Italian. I'm Italian. Close family, you know. I live now on the same street I grew up on."

"In the same house?"

"No." She sighed, as though trying to remove a weight from her chest. "A few houses down. My mother still lives in the old house. My father died when I was thirteen."

"Brothers and sisters?"

"Two sisters. One older. One younger."

"Do they live nearby?"

"The older one does. She's married. Has a family. They live across the street from the old house. The younger one is away at school in Vermont. She doesn't come home much."

"What about you? Did you go to college?"

"No. I was never a student type, if you know what I mean. I did okay in school and like that, but when I got out of high school I'd sort of had it with . . . I don't know. I just didn't want any more. Anyway, I got pregnant."

"How old were you?"

"When I got pregnant?"

"Yes."

"I was eighteen. Just eighteen."

"Did your mother know? Your sisters?"

"Oh yeah. My mother had a fit. Everybody had a fit. My family's very emotional. Very religious. The whole neighborhood is like that. I mean you're supposed to be a virgin until you get married and all. I almost ran away rather than have anybody know, but . . ."–two lines of tension formed between her eyebrows–"where would I go? Anyway, it all came out and my mother said if my father was alive he'd kill me. It's more likely he would have killed Bill."

"Bill was the father?"

"Yes."

"How many times did you sleep with him before you became pregnant?"

"I never did sleep with him before we were married. We did it in cars and places, you know. I guess it was about, I don't know, maybe ten times."

"Was Bill your first?"

"Yes."

"And you married him?"

"Well, I was pregnant."

"What kind of person was your husband?"

"He was older than me, thirteen years older. He was a car mechanic and people said he was good at it, except he drank a lot. We never really got together but anyway I got pregnant again. The first was a boy and the second a girl. Bill never even came to the hospital for the second one. He was drunk."

"How did you feel about that?"

"I don't know. I was confused about him because he beat me up from time to time and when I got home he started again and it was really bad. Anyway we were married eight years and I tried to kill myself."

"How?"

"Sleeping pills. My mother found me and after that I divorced Bill and he took off and no one has seen him since, but he does send money. You know, just enough to keep me from pressing charges of nonsupport."

"How old are the children now?"

"The kids? The kids are fourteen and sixteen."

"You say Bill was the first. How was sex with Bill?"

"Hard. He liked to do it hard, you know. He liked to bruise me."

"Did you like it?"

"Sometimes I did. I was so lonely that just to be with someone . . . you know?"

"Did you have sex with anyone while you were married to Bill?"

"Oh, no. Never."

"Why?"

"I was married. I mean I was home. I was married, my mother right down the street. There was no way."

"Did you think about other men?"

"No."

"Did you love Bill?"

"I could have maybe if he didn't drink. No, I don't think I did."

"How did life go after the divorce? I mean your sex life."

"At first there wasn't much 'cause, you know, I was getting over Bill and all that. But then I started going out with guys."

"How was it?"

"It was all right except I would freeze up when they wanted to do it."

"Did you do it?"

"I did it sometimes but I could never feel anything."

"Is that still true?"

"I haven't been to bed or anything with a man for over a year. A few months ago I went to a resort for Christmas and I met this man I kind of liked but we, or I . . . I don't know, it just never happened."

"Do you like men sexually?"

"Yes I do. I just find it hard to relax."

"Do you masturbate?"

"Not so much."

"When you do, what do you think of?"

"Bodies."

"What types of bodies?"

"My own kind of. Women's bodies. I don't know."

"Do you ever think of men?"

"Yes. I mean, I think of doing it with a man too but . . . I don't know. Sometimes I don't think of anything."

"Is it difficult not having someone to make love with?"

"I do have someone. I have Rita."

"Tell me about Rita."

"She's my closest friend. I've known her about eight years. She's very strong. I don't mean strong like muscles or anything but strong with her kids and her husband. She really runs her house. Nobody puts anything over on Rita. We're both about the same age. I'm a year older."

"You and Rita are lovers?"

"I guess you'd call it that. She loves me anyway. About two years ago she started to make advances and she convinced me to go to bed with her."

"She convinced you?"

"Well, yeah. I didn't really want to but it's hard to say no to Rita. She usually gets what she wants."

"How often do you have sex with Rita?"

"Whenever she wants. About once a week, I guess."

"Do you enjoy it?"

"I do sometimes. I enjoy it while we're doing it but after I feel mixed up. Guilt, like I shouldn't be doing it."

"Why do you do it?"

"I'm afraid if I don't Rita will . . . not come around anymore."

"Desert you?"

"Something like that."

"Could you live without Rita?"

"I don't think so. Rita . . . she picks out my clothes, if I want to go somewhere she drives me. I'm afraid of trains. I'm afraid to be alone when I travel even just back and forth to shop. I just can't take care of myself, I guess, you know? I don't know what I'd do without Rita."

"Do you consider yourself dependent?"

"I guess so. Like I once told my younger sister, as long as Bill told me what to do things were all right. And she said I was too dependent. The rougher Bill was on me the more it excited me. Like a really nice man doesn't turn me on. My sister said I was masochistic. Is that what you call it?"

"Is Rita rough on you?"

"Sexually?"

"Yes."

"She's pretty rough, I guess.

"Do you like it?"

"It excites me how excited she gets. I need Rita. I get depressed a lot and Rita snaps me out of it."

"Do you think of yourself as bisexual?"

"Rita says I am."

"What do you think?"

"I guess I must be."

"Are you interested in other women?"

"More and more I am but I haven't done it with other women. It makes me feel guilty."

"What about men? Do you feel guilty with men?"

"Yes, but in a different way. It seems more natural but I don't know. Sex has always made me feel sort of bad after."

There is a relatively happy ending to Nora's story. Through therapy she became more assertive and aware of her own needs, and less dependent on other people's wishes and unhealthy needs.

Before therapy Nora had become a troubled human being whose bisexuality was still another way to reinforce masochistic and dependent tendencies. With a very low self-image, she used her bisexuality to punish herself doubly for wanting sex in any manner at all. Her lovers, male and female, took her in sex as though she had no will of her own. She *is* bisexual but she couldn't handle its complexity, its ambiguity, and she was, I felt, probably better off (considering her values) with one male lover, but a tender and understanding one. She is now living in a southern city with a quiet man who loves her. In time, as her confidence grows, she might be ready for a relationship with a woman. In our correspondence since the close of therapy, she says that though still attracted to women she is faithful to the man who has become her second husband.

Walter D.

I first met Walter at a meeting of the Bisexual Forum in New York City. The members of the Bisexual Forum met once a week in the late 1970s and early '80s for the purpose of discussing bisexuality and meeting other bisexuals socially. After giving a talk on the subject of sexual dysfunction and orientation, I asked if there were any questions from the audience.

"Do you think the size of a man's penis has any bearing on his ability as a lover?" was one question asked by a tall middle-aged man, who identified himself as Walter D. of New Orleans, Louisiana.

The audience groaned. Their disapproval wasn't, I felt, meant to be unkind. This is a question that has been asked and answered so often that to hear it again was more than those assembled could bear. It's still a good question, though. The answer, "It doesn't matter," is true only to the degree that penis size doesn't matter to those involved in the sexual encounter. It *can* affect sexual performance if it is allowed to–the mind being the most sensitive erogenous zone of all.

Before I could answer, one young woman stood up and said that although her boyfriend had the smallest penis she had ever seen, he had "a pile-driving ass."

Well, that brought the house down and the meeting to a close. Later, over wine and cheese, Walter apologized for the question. I told him that there was no need for apology and that he had every right to ask any question that came to mind.

"Listen," he said, "I don't want to commit myself to therapy right now because I'll be going back to Louisiana in a month or so, but I would like to talk to you."

We set up an appointment and I saw him for four sessions on a consultation basis, to review his problems and explore his possible choices for the future.

"You don't have a southern accent," I observed, after turning on the tape. "Are you from Louisiana originally?"

"No, originally I'm from Chicago. My parents are from Louisiana. They moved back when I was fourteen."

"How was that?"

"It was okay. I wasn't too crazy about Chicago."

"How old are you, Walter?"

"Forty-six."

"Did your work bring you to New York?"

"Yes. I work for an airline. I'm based in New York for a while. Actually I'm trying to get into public relations again. That's what I did before I went to work for the airline."

"Why did you leave P.R. work?"

"About three years ago my wife died of pneumonia. It was so sudden I guess I went to pieces. We had two children. They're sixteen and eighteen now–a boy and a girl. I lost my job and when I recovered, a friend got me the airline job. I took it for the kids and because it was the only offer I had at the time."

"Did you have a good relationship with your wife?"

"I'd say so."

"Do you mind talking about it?"

"No."

"Did you have a satisfactory sex life with her?"

"The thing is I should tell you now that I left her a few months before she died. Actually about eight months before she died."

"You said it was a good relationship."

"It was for what it was, but I met this guy Ken and we fell in love and I just moved out on Bonny. . . ."

"How long were you and Bonny married?"

"Seventeen years."

"Did she know about your bisexuality?"

"The last few years she did."

"Did she accept it?"

"No. That's why we had to split, I think. It was more than she could handle. She wanted me to give up guys. There was no way I was going to do that."

"You say you went to pieces when your wife died. Were you sorry you had left her?"

"No, but I felt guilty. If I hadn't left she might not have died, and all that. Then there were the kids. They knew I left to live with a guy. My daughter ran away. Ran away three times until my mother came to live with us. Then Ken and I broke up. There was just too much going on and he got fed up. Then I lost my job. It was a nightmare, all of it."

"Do you get along with your mother?"

"Better since my father died, but she hates my lifestyle. My father hated it more. He was really bad news. We were always going for each other's eyes. I never could win with him. He was a man's man and he used to call me a pansy and stuff like that. He was cruel to my mother. I wasted no tears when he died, believe me. To tell you the truth my whole family is a pain in the ass, including my older brother and my kid sister. I haven't seen them in years. They're married, living in California. The only good thing about them is they didn't like my father either. I'm the only one who gets along with my mother. She was pretty good to me and the kids when Bonny died. It was mainly because of her, though, that I lost Ken. He couldn't take her sarcasm. I didn't blame him. I can barely stand it myself."

"How is your relationship with your children now?"

"With the boy it's not so hot. But my daughter and I are good friends now. I guess I'm closer to her than I am to anybody these days. She understands me. She stopped running away and she's accepted my bisexuality."

"How long have you been bisexual, from your point of view?"

"You mean when did I start turning on to guys?"

"Were you turned on to women first?"

"Yes, I guess I was. I liked girls at first. Then, about sixteen, I got into guys too."

"Let's begin at the beginning. Did you masturbate when you were a boy?"

"Yes."

"How old were you when you began?"

"About ten or eleven."

"Did you fantasize?"

"Yes, but I began having sex really when I was five or six in the garage at home. Neighborhood kids playing doctor and nurse type of thing."

"Did you experience orgasm at that time?"

"I don't think so. The first orgasm was when I was ten, as I said, and then the first real sex I had with another person was in a gang bang when I was twelve. We called the girl–she was about fifteen– the town pump. She put out for everybody. Then we used to have circle jerks among the boys to see who could come first. That used to fascinate me."

"Do you still masturbate?"

"Sure. Every day."

"What do you fantasize about?"

"Guys mostly. To tell you the truth, women put me uptight. See, I have a small cock. I enjoy the company of women but . . . the woman I most enjoyed sexually was my wife. We really had good sex. She was a virgin when we married and so I knew she wasn't comparing my cock to other guys! I felt secure with her in bed."

"Did you enjoy all kinds of sex with her?"

"No. She used to want to go down on me but I don't like it when a woman does that. And I don't like to go down on a woman."

"How about men?"

"Oh, I like to have a guy go down on me and I like to rim and suck a guy off. But a woman, no. I like to just, you know, feel and fuck a woman."

"Have you had any relationships with women since your wife?"

"A few. One I met in Florida. I bought this share in a house for the spring and summer and she was there too. I never should have gotten involved with her."

"Why?"

"She was the aggressive type. I was okay the first time we had sex on the beach at night, but the second time I was impotent. She was one of these really horny women who just come on so strong, but in bed her body was so, I don't know, tense with need, so demanding, that I had to. . . . You know when a woman keeps moving up on the bed when you start fucking her. . . . Well, she was just all over the place, and pushing her pelvis up and just getting all she could out of me before I was really ready. She just wanted to have sex, I guess, just to get off. It was awful. Anyway, I lost my erection. We made it after that but she wanted to suck my cock and there is just something piggy to me when a woman does that. I lose respect for her. Don't misunderstand, I know this is my hang-up, but that's the kind of hairpin I am."

"Do you have a relationship going now with a man or a woman?"

"No. But I have sex a lot. With guys. I get turned on once in a while to a woman though. Recently I spent time with this guy from Arizona State, where we went to college together years ago. I was in this car accident and got some money and went there to college. That was one of the best times of my whole life. I was freshman president, had a part-time job in a gay bar and was really close to this guy there. Anyway, we got together lately and it was good. He was straight when I met him. One of the things I really love to do is to bring a straight guy out. Anyway, while he was here we went dancing–I love to dance–and made it all over again. But he's gone back now. I'll see him again, though, I'm sure of that. I've also met a woman recently whom I like. I don't know."

"What don't you know?"

"I don't know."

"Would you describe yourself as a happy person, Walter?"

"Sure. I think I am. Sure I am. Why not? I got nothing to complain about these days. Sure I'm happy. But I know things are not completely right. There are times at night when I don't sleep that I get these glimpses of myself that I realize are all messed up. And I am confused about my relationships, about men, about women. I'm generally happy, but I'd like to get rid of the confusion. . . ."

Walter is confused, and I would be surprised if he really is as happy as he claims to be. His view of himself is negative, his relationship with both men and women is generally not fulfilling, and his sexuality is full of aversions and compulsions. He uses sex to work out other needs. His preoccupation with his "small penis" is symbolic of his view of himself. When questioned in detail, he admitted that his penis is of average length. On further questioning, he admitted that his sex with men also is full of problems. I strongly recommended to him that he seek therapy in Louisiana as soon as he settled down, which he did. Walter's bisexuality was part and parcel of his generally problematic functioning; his sexuality in general was only one aspect of his poor relationships.

Ann C.

I came to Ann's story in a most unconventional way. One weekend in early summer I invited some friends up to my summer home in the mountains of New York State. One of them, Edwin, called to ask if he could bring along a girl he'd recently met and was involved with.

"I've only known her three weeks," he said, "but we're at that point where we just can't stand to be apart. She's very vulnerable, kind of haunted, like a bird with a broken wing. She won't be any trouble."

I thought Edwin's description was fairly accurate–she was vulnerable and apparently broken, at least in her capacity to reason.

It rained on Saturday. I think that had as much to do with what followed as anything else. Because of the weather, a kind of cabin fever took hold. I wasn't bothered myself by the confinement because it gave me an opportunity to work. But, in retrospect, I should have been a more responsible host.

About three o'clock on this truly dismal afternoon I heard a crashing sound, followed by silence. Then such angry voices were raised that I left my room, walked down the hall to Edwin's door, and knocked.

There was no answer. I didn't knock again but went down to the kitchen for a cup of coffee. A few minutes later Edwin rushed by me, suitcase in hand. Before I could speak he was in his car backing out the driveway. He did stop halfway, as though considering his action, but as he explained later he was too full of anger to say goodbye. ("Honestly," he explained in a phone conversation the following Monday, "I was afraid if I stayed one more minute I'd kill her.")

I poured two cups of coffee and went upstairs. Ann was sitting at the foot of the bed staring down at a ceramic lamp that lay in half a dozen rather neat pieces at her feet.

"I hope it wasn't an antique," she said.

"I wasn't attached to it, if that's what you mean." I handed her a cup of coffee. "Do you like it black?"

"Thank you." She took the cup but her hand was trembling.

"Here." I took it from her, putting it on the dresser.

"Is he gone?"

"It appears he is."

"Christ." Tears began to roll down her cheeks.

"Do you want to tell me what happened?"

She did. She told me over the next hour, though there is no way my memory could accurately record her exact words. As her story unfolded I saw in her what appeared to be a psychosexual confusion so profound that I suggested she take a nap before we talked any further.

"Are you just putting me off?" she asked.

"No."

"I would like to talk," she said, "though I should catch the next bus back to the city."

"That's not necessary," I told her. "We'll talk after dinner. Would you mind if I recorded our conversation?"

"No. As long as I can talk. But why?"

"Your situation, your problems, could be of help to other people. I won't use your real name, and the particulars of your life will be disguised. In short, your identity won't be compromised."

In all we spent three hours talking, the last talk taking place in my car as we drove back to the city on Sunday evening.

Ann is an attractive young woman, although her looks are very much subject to the way she's feeling. She was feeling good when we were talking. It occurred to me that she looked like the women in those movies who have to take off their glasses in order to become "beautiful." What follows is the essence of our talks.

"How old are you, Ann?"

"Twenty-eight."

"Tell me about your background."

"I come from Bridgehampton, Long Island. I live there with my mother and my grandmother. Usually in the winter I go to Florida and come back to Bridgehampton for the summer. I've been doing that for years. That's where I met Edwin. We met on the beach and just started talking. I had just gotten back from a really lousy winter in Florida and . . . I was horny. We were having sex within an hour after we met. Trouble is, I didn't come. I have trouble coming. He just wasn't doing it the way I need it done. That's why he stormed out this afternoon."

"What happened?"

"We started having sex and I got terribly excited and I bit him. I guess I bit him too hard because he hit me. That really turned me on and I sort of got him pissed so he'd really get on me. Really put it to me. But it didn't get him excited, it just got him angry. So I got angry and hit him across the face. Then I told him about this guy I slept with in Florida who I always could come with, which was true, but that's when he broke the lamp. I knew I shouldn't have said it but I was horny. I'm always horny. I think it throws people off because I don't look like the sexy type."

"Earlier you told me a bit about how you were with your mother and grandmother. Could you go into that again, but in more detail?"

"Where do you want me to begin?"

"Wherever you're comfortable."

"My family owns this big restaurant in the Hamptons. That is, they did own it until two years ago when they sold it. I still think of it as ours, though it's closed now. The new owner couldn't make a go of it. It was such a success when we had it because of my grandmother, who's the best German cook anywhere. But she wanted to retire. She's eighty-two now."

"Did your mother work in the restaurant?"

"We all did. My grandmother, my mother, my older brother, and myself."

"What about your father?"

"Boy, there's a question. I never knew him. Never saw him. I don't know to this day if he's alive or dead. My mother divorced him a few months after I was born. He was Irish. My mother and grandmother are German."

"Let's talk about your sex life. What was your first sexual experience?"

"Masturbating."

"How old were you when you began?"

"About six."

"Can you describe what you did? What you thought about? How you viewed it?"

"It sort of all comes together, if you'll pardon the pun. Like from six to sixteen I masturbated and it was the only sex I had till then. My favorite way was to be alone in the house–I first did this when I was eight–and put on my mother's bra and stuff it with napkins or Kleenex. I'd put on her makeup and a slip and parade in front of the mirror until I got really hot and then I would get a hand mirror and get on the bed and hold the mirror between my legs and masturbate with my finger. I did that a lot. A couple of times a week. I'd be so afraid I'd get caught and I was so guilty. I mean, I felt guilty all the time."

"Did you have fantasies when you masturbated?"

"Yes. I would think about breasts. Women's breasts. I still do. The thought of breasts really gets me off. I wish I had big ones so I could suck my own."

"Does that happen as well when you're with a man? Do you think of women's breasts?"

"Not always. Just sometimes."

"In our previous conversation you said you were bisexual."

"Yes. For the first time. I was in therapy in Florida for a time and that was the first time I ever told *anyone* I masturbated or how I masturbated. It's only over the past few months I realized I'm bisexual although I've always known it in a way. I used to think that maybe I was a lesbian."

"Let's hold on a minute now and go back to when you were sixteen. That's when you first had sex with another person?"

"Yes."

"Male?"

"Yes. This boy from high school."

"How was that?"

"Better for him than me, I think. I just never got off. I used to go home after and masturbate."

"Were there other men after that?"

"Until I was eighteen I went out with quite a few boys. Then one night two boys gave me a ride home from school. It was spring and pretty warm out. We went to the beach and I made it with both of them. I came. It was the first time I'd ever come with another person but I really felt . . . like I thought I must be some kind of pig. I felt that's what the boys thought."

"Did you see them again?"

"Not sexually. When I graduated from high school I cracked up."

"What do you mean 'cracked up'?"

"I just went to pieces. I felt like my mother and my grandmother were trying to destroy me. I really felt that. I began having tantrums and smashing things and just going crazy at home. And then one day my mother, who's a very cool, cold person, and I were in the kitchen and for no immediate reason I turned on her. I grabbed her around the throat and I tried to strangle her. I really wanted to kill her. My brother came running in and pried me off her. I kept saying, 'Why don't you love me? Why don't you love me?' Then I just fell apart after my brother made me apologize. To this day I hate that he did that. Made me apologize."

"Why?"

"I don't know. I just felt so alone when he made me tell her I was sorry, because I wasn't sorry. She never did love me. They tell me I look like my father. My mother and grandmother hate my father. I think they must hate me too. People tell me I look Irish. Everyone else in my family looks German. Anyway, they sent me away to this expensive beautiful funny farm and I was there for a year. I was twenty when I got out. I didn't go to college. I took odd jobs cleaning people's summer houses but in the winter there was no work so I went to Florida and waitressed. I've been doing that now for six years. Back and forth and every spring when I come north I go home to my mother and grandmother. They put me down all the time. Nothing I do is right, although my grandmother and I are closer now."

"Why do you go back?"

"Money. I can never make enough money to make it on my own. My family is pretty rich. My brother is off on his own now. Very successful in business. He never goes back. He told me recently that he understands now why I am the way I am. They treated him better than they treated me because he was a boy and because he looks like them. I swear in that house with those two women I'm a freak."

"What if you *had* to survive on your own financially?"

"I know what you're getting at. It's not the money I go back for. It's the pain. I've heard all that before."

"Is it true?"

"Listen, you can't live without money. I can never make enough to get away."

"Would you if you could?"

"I'd rather not pursue that if you don't mind."

"All right, Ann. Tell me, if you will, the pattern of your love life over the past six years."

"After I got out of the funny farm I met quite a few men but nothing came of it except I just felt more frustration. In spite of my sexual drive I don't want much more in bed than to be screwed and to come. For instance I'm not into oral sex. My jaw gets tired sucking a man and I don't much like being eaten. I like to be fingered. I like to be kissed and fingered at the same time. That always gets me off. I like it when a man puts his cock between my legs. I get very excited over that. I don't know why. Men tell me I don't do enough in bed. I like the man to take me away, if you know what I mean.

"Last winter I met this man in Florida. We had wonderful sex. I always came with him. Not much foreplay. We really had good sex and a lot of it. Then one day I came home early from work and he was dressed up in my clothes. A dress, wig, makeup, everything. At first I was shocked, but he told me he does it all the time. He has a wardrobe of women's clothes and he gets some kind of release from dressing that way. What bothered me was that here at last was a man who satisfied me sexually, and he liked to dress as a woman. He said—and this man is in his mid-forties—that his secret desire is to be a lesbian. He's a successful architect and no fool but he has lots of problems with his father. It really confused me and we broke up before I left. You know I told you that I had this thing about women's breasts. He told me he'd get hormone shots so he'd have breasts for me. I almost said yes. Can you imagine? I really considered it. Then I went into therapy for a while and the therapist suggested I try a woman just to see if I really did want that. I never went back to him after that but I thought a lot about it. When I came back north about two months ago I had a dream about sex with a woman. I woke up crying. Not that it was a nightmare. It wasn't. It was just so good. The next night I went to this gay bar out on the highway. It's a lesbian bar. I'd known about it for years. Sure enough I got into this conversation with a woman about ten years older than me. She had big breasts and she was a very warm person. I was nervous of course because the bar is not that far from the house I grew up in, but I wanted the experience so badly that it didn't matter. The woman made a date with me, which I didn't keep, but I went back to the bar a couple of times and on one of them I met her again. We went for a drive in my car and she kissed me when I let her off at the bar again. We made another date and *finally* wound up in bed. She had really large breasts, not terribly firm, but she let me play with them and I sucked them and cried and just sucked them and played with them like some thirsty person off a desert. She fingered me and I came and after a few more dates I fingered her but she wanted to sixty-nine with me and that turned me away. I met another woman at the bar with really beautiful breasts and nipples and I've been seeing her a lot. Her name is Lola and we have a good time. We had a fight last week because I've been seeing Edwin too. That's why I came on this weekend, to punish her because she's been mean to me lately."

"In what way mean to you?"

"She says I should leave my mother and grandmother and that I'm weak. I can't stand it when someone says I'm weak."

"Do you think you are strong?"

"No. But I just don't like anyone to think of me as weak. Lola wants me to move in with her and share the rent and so on. She's really been nice and we get off good together. But I don't want to be a lesbian."

"What do you want to be?"

"Straight, I guess. Or maybe bisexual, but I don't want to be a lesbian. Yet I need the love I get from Lola."

"How does it compare to the love you get from Edwin?"

"You know the thing about who would you save in a burning building? Well, in a burning building I'd save Lola."

I could come out with some diagnostic words and label Ann, but that's not my purpose here. What is important is to be able to see how her involvement with others on a psychosexual level is streaked with hurts, ambivalences, nonrealistic strivings and internal expectations. Her bisexual nature is not as important as her need to be hurt, her desire for fetishistic objects, her confusion and very low self-image. She functions poorly on almost all levels. As a bisexual, her relationships with both men and women leave a good deal to be desired both on a sexual as well as an emotional plane. Her feelings of being unloved affect her ability to love others–both men and women. On parting she told me that she plans to enter therapy again when she returns to Florida in the winter. Let's hope that the pain of being considered a "freak" is diminished, or perhaps even eliminated altogether.

Donald J.

Donald J. is a 27-year-old pediatric resident in one of the New York hospitals, undergoing psychoanalytic psychotherapy. Born in Montreal, Canada, the youngest of four in a close-knit Jewish family, he had his first sexual exchange with a female prostitute at the age of 18. This was followed by several similar experiences, none of which he found fulfilling. At 22 he was "fulfilled" when he began a good sexual relationship with a girl he met in medical school in Toronto. It lasted for a year and a half. During this time he carried on an "unfulfilling" sexual relationship with a male medical student as well, although he remembers the relationship itself– its emotional content–as more satisfying than the one with the girl. After these two alliances ended he formed another male relationship in which the sex was excellent but the emotional relatedness all but nonexistent. This relationship ended when he moved to New York for his internship.

Living in New York the past two years, Donald fell into an active homosexual life. He visited bars, went weekly to the gay baths and formed mostly gay friendships. I say he "fell into" this life because he has shown in his history more expansive possibilities. But an incident of impotency with a woman, on arriving in New York, activated his underlying unconscious fear of women. Donald began to avoid them, and his superficial male relationships were hardly fulfilling.

His major problem is combining sex with an otherwise good relationship. He's proved a capacity for both, but not with the same person. He wants to marry and have children, at the same time leaving open the possibility of one or two male friends or lovers. Therapy has helped him understand some of his neurotic behavior; recently he has begun to spend most of his time with a female social worker. His impotence has not returned and I feel he is open to the possibility of complete intimacy–this time combining sex and intimacy in the same relationship, male or female.

Because I feel Donald is more than halfway out of the tunnel of neurosis he has moved through all of his life, and still going strong, his progress is difficult to pinpoint. He is a troubled bisexual but he is becoming healthy by changing. As an illustration, I offer a short conversation that recently took place in my office:

"The last time we talked," I said, "you spoke of marriage. How do you feel about that now?"

"Good. 'Stronger' would be a better word. Millie [the social worker] is sure but I'm still feeling my way. She doesn't really understand the fear I have of the impotence returning."

"Has it?"

"No. But it's there in the sense that I worry about it. And then there is the homosexual thing. I've told Millie about it but she doesn't take it seriously. I don't think she cares if I go to bed with a man because she really can't *imagine* it. Now with another woman I know she'd be upset because she told me so."

"Do you see your bisexuality as a problem?"

"I want men. I want Millie and I want men. How can I tell Millie that one of the great joys of my life is getting down on my knees and sucking a big beautiful cock? I still spend a lot of time looking for the big and bigger cock to suck."

"Is that a problem?"

"It will be if I lose Millie."

"Is that likely? Is that a *real* fear?"

"No. I see what you're asking. No, it's not. I'm still confused about which . . . I mean what I want. On my knees with that cock in my mouth, I don't have to be really responsible except to give pleasure. Does that make any sense?"

"What about getting pleasure . . . direct pleasure?"

"I get direct pleasure with Millie, but I don't trust it. I don't trust it to *be* there. Does that mean I don't trust women?"

"What do you think?"

"Let me tell you what I think you think. Okay?"

"Sure."

"It's not that I don't trust women. It's that I don't trust myself with women. Did I ring the bell?"

"Did you hear it?"

"Yes."

"So did I." I laughed.

I won't go into the dynamics of some of Donald's homosexual behavior except to say that he has worked out a good deal in therapy and is now able to be not only sexually intimate with another male but also emotionally intimate. His compulsions have lessened or disappeared as he has matured. In fact, we are about to end therapy. Donald's relationship with Millie has also progressed to the point where they are living together and are making plans for marriage. As a matter of fact it would now not be inappropriate to transfer Donald to the next chapter–"The Healthy Bisexual." However, his "health" is quite new and not yet deeply entrenched, so let's leave him here as a person in transition.

Chapter 7

The Healthy Bisexual–
Profiles

I once had a patient who through a hellish compact with his conscience held a locked-up point of view on all things sexual. It took very little to engage his conscience, and one day he struck his wife when she suggested that his point of view had more to do with intolerance than it did with common sense. She left him, taking their four-year-old son with her.

"It broke my heart," he said at our first session. "It's a goddamn crime these days to have a healthy say about sex."

"What is 'a healthy say'?" I asked.

"We had our son in this private school, and I found out that not only were some of the teachers homosexual but the head mistress . . . the *head mistress* was a dyke."

"Was she a good headmistress?"

"What the hell difference does that make? She was sick. How can you be a good anything if you're sick?"

"How do you know she was sick?"

"What do you mean, how do I know?"

"Did she do anything to indicate to you that she was sick?"

"That's what my wife asked before I hit her."

"Is that why you hit her?"

"Listen, I'm not proud of the fact I hit her, but don't tell me anyone can do a good job at anything if they're unable to have a normal sex life."

"I would never tell you that."

"Then I'm right."

"By definition, yes."

"Why couldn't she see that?"

"Maybe she did," I said as gently as possible.

"Then why did I hit her?" He began shaking his head. "No. No. That's not what I mean. I mean why. . . . " And he sat in the chair in genuine bewilderment for the next couple of minutes. . . .

His confusion is common. In a democratic society if the majority believes blue is green, chances are that blue will soon come to be green. Majority opinion is a powerful means of persuasion. But as we know, the majority is not always right.

When my patient hit his wife he was speaking for the primeval past. When she walked out of the house, she was speaking, silently, for a more enlightened present and future. "Then why did I hit her?" he asked. And before drawing another breath he had an inkling of why. Although he couldn't at the moment realize it, the "truth" stunned him. We are, in our time, not only undergoing rapid changes in our understanding of human sexuality but in our understanding of all areas of human thought. Less than a decade this side of the year 2000, we can for the first time in human history afford to admit that women are equal to men and that sexuality is a means of creative expression as well as an instinctual procreative drive.

The healthy bisexual is a twentieth-century idea. What can we learn from the healthy bisexual? I offer the following cases.

Harold G.

For the first edition of this book, I interviewed Harold G. in 1976-once in my office and twice at his apartment on Manhattan's Central Park West. Harold is a successful television writer whose work has earned him a reputation for what is called in the trade "quality product." The most striking thing about him physically was how young he appeared for his 55 years.

"You don't look a day over forty," I said at our first meeting.

"It's in the genes, I guess."

"You don't think it's perhaps *how* you lived?"

"Oh sure. But one tends to play down such . . . well, vanity."

"Are you vain?"

"Not vain, but perhaps a bit unblushing when it comes to what I have."

"Have you always been so sure of yourself?"

"No."

"What kind of background have you had?"

"You want the long version or the short?" He shook his head and smiled. "No, no, I'm kidding. I was born in Philadelphia in what I suppose you'd call a semi-slum. My mother died when I was about eight. My father was a fender repairman. He ran an orthodox Jewish home for me and two older brothers. We were eight, fourteen, and sixteen. My oldest brother left home when he was about twenty, and he later became a playwright. Very successful. Very respected. Very famous. He changed his name."

"Is that why you became a writer?"

"Yes and no. I'd wanted to be a doctor, but there wasn't enough money. Besides, World War II decided a lot of things. I was drafted and served five years. The war was hell, as they say, and when it was over, I wanted to be really free. I was good at writing so that's what I did. I was in on the early days of television and I grew with it."

"Any regrets?"

"Yes, in the sense that I'm not the artist my brother is, but then again the quality of my life is and has been more nicely balanced than his. I'm happy. He's not. 'Happy' is a dumb word, but I think you know what 1 mean."

"Why are you 'happy' and why isn't he?"

"We've talked about it. We have a good relationship. He's gay. Really locked into the life and, like anybody locked in, he's kind of desperate. My other brother–the middle one–became a lawyer, a very good one. He's married, living in Arizona. Straight as an arrow and we don't get along at all. He's been married three times, by the way, whatever that says. He won't talk to my oldest brother at all because of the homosexual thing. Weird."

"Tell me about your sex life. When did you first experience sex?"

"I actually remember getting this great feeling when I played with myself, as early as two or three. Continued to do so, which naturally turned into masturbation. Never had any wet dreams because I never missed a day."

"Guilt?"

"Sure, but not enough to stop me. When I got older I used to forge notes so I could get sex books from the library. My brothers helped me, too. We all read a lot. Not just sex books. Everything."

"What fantasy life did you have?"

"General thoughts of women. Pinups. Betty Grable. You know. I began playing around with girls when I was about eleven or twelve. Nothing heavy but lots of feeling and kissing."

"Did you like it?"

"Oh sure."

"Did you have anything sexually to do with males at that time?"

"Not unless you count circle jerks at camp, and then there was this kid on the block in Philly who used to blow everybody."

"Did you like that?"

"Yes, but I didn't admit it, even to myself."

"Why not?"

"I didn't want to be thought of as queer. I didn't want to think of myself that way. And I knew my oldest brother was homosexual. He left the neighborhood, but still everybody knew my father threw him out of the house. So I thought that being queer was dangerous. Then my other brother, the lawyer, became *super* straight. I suppose to make my father happy. It really screwed him up. My father used to say that my mother would turn over in her grave if she knew her first born was 'a sissy boy.' So the second born had to make up for that. It was hard on him, and he used to warn me of the dangers of becoming 'a pervert' like our older brother."

"Did you think of your oldest brother as a pervert?"

"No. I thought he was terrific. But I didn't say that. Jesus, it was worth my life at home to say a kind word about 'the faygela,' and the neighborhood was just as bad."

"How old were you when you had your first sexual encounter with a woman?"

"Oh that. Boy, that was awful. A gang-bang. I must have been like tenth in line. I was seventeen. I never saw the girl's face. She was kneeling up on a bed, and guys were lined up outside this window of a closed-up summer cottage. She was taking it in the vagina from behind. Lots of guys lined up. Really sordid but not unusual. That went on a lot in those days. There were those girls who would do it in a gang-bang. My lawyer brother sort of made me do it. Then he went home and he told my father I was a man, and that made my father happy. I was about to be drafted, and they both wanted to get me laid first so I would . . . 'get off on the right foot.'"

"How was the army sexually?"

"That's when I began my sex life, really. I met a girl after boot camp, and it took a while but I finally got her in bed. I was going overseas, and that took care of her guilt, I suppose. Anyway it had that love-in-a-sleeping-bag quality, and we had quite a lovely time, although neither of us knew what we were doing. She was a nice girl. We talked a lot. Then I left. I was gone for nearly five years so, although we didn't know it at the time, that was the end of that."

"You went overseas?"

"Yes. I won't go into my experience in the war more than to tell you I was a lab tech and a medic. I got my doctor thing out doing that. What I didn't lose was my interest in psychology. In fact, I sometimes ghost as a writer for psychological articles. I know quite a bit about psychology, for a layman. Anyway, my work in the army brought me close to nurses, and although they weren't supposed to socialize with enlisted men, they did and I managed to get close to a few."

"Sexually?"

"Yes. They were all, without exception, older than I was. Some only a few years, some as much as ten or twelve. The longest relationship was with a woman thirty-two. I was nineteen. We had to sneak around because of the regulations. We had very intense sex because it was all we could have, and I learned a great deal from her. She was the first woman I ever made love to who had an orgasm when we fucked. I thought that was so wonderful. Before that I didn't know women were supposed to enjoy it. She *enjoyed* it. Everything. I remember once in London we managed to find a room for twenty-four hours. She got there before I did, and when I went into the room she was lying on the bed naked. Her long, beautiful legs spread, her hands cupped around her breasts, and written across her belly in lipstick was 'MATINEE TODAY.' "

"Did you feel anything like love for her?"

"In a way, but not deeply. I might have but they shipped her out. Back to the States, I think. I missed her very much.

"For about six months I didn't have sex with anyone. Then I met Stan. He was a chaplain's assistant. He played classical piano and was an incredibly sensitive human being. Very good looking. Older than I was–I'd say about twenty-eight. We met off the base at some beer party. At first we were just friends. I knew he was homosexual but I figured I could handle it."

"Were you attracted to him?"

"I didn't think I was. I just didn't think of myself as being attracted to men. Well, we got a twenty-four-hour pass at the same time and we went into London. Took a room together. That night in bed he reached over and touched me. Before I knew it he was down on me. I wanted to stop him but it felt so good. And it was exciting to be desired that way. He went down on me about three times during the night. Each time it got better. In the morning he was asleep so I skipped out. Back at the base I wouldn't talk to him, and after a few days I asked for a transfer. I got it. I never saw him again."

"Were you bothered by the incident?"

"Haunted by it. I swore I'd never do that again."

"Did you think you'd turn out like your oldest brother?"

"Exactly."

"Did you do it again?"

"Not till 1950. I was discharged and went to New York University on the G.I. Bill. I met a girl there at one of the dances. We fell in love, made plans to get married and did get married within the year. June 1946. We've been married now thirty years. Her name is Alice."

"Is it a good marriage?"

"I think so."

"Children?"

"One. A son. He's married, living in Florida. Good kid."

"How often do you and your wife make love?"

"You mean over the past thirty years? That's a tough question. I would say two-three times a week. She had rheumatic fever as a child and has a heart condition, which sometimes gets in the way. We have good sex, though."

"Have you had other women over the past thirty years?"

For the first time he hesitated before answering. "No." He sat quietly for a while. "I've wanted to but I'm terribly romantic when it comes to women. I could easily think I've fallen in love and I just don't want to hurt Alice. Also, I have this impotence thing with women the first time. I had it with the nurse and that first girl and Alice–every women I've ever slept with. I never thought of it as a problem. I still don't. I've never been impotent with any woman more than once, the first time. But that makes it hard–no pun intended–to make it with other women unless I develop a relationship, and I'm very involved with Alice so it's just never happened. There have been two episodes over the years, but neither went beyond that first impotent time. The thing is, with a woman I have to *know* her. I have to care."

"Do you see that as a hang-up?"

"Yes, but I think it's a good one. It means I value sex with women." He smiled. "Also I'm smart enough to know that that's a rationalization. It's generational, I think. How I was brought up."

"Had you forgotten about Stan by the time you got married?"

"I thought I had. But of course I hadn't. Then in 1950 I was walking the dog in Riverside Park at night. This guy approached me and we went into the bushes. He blew me. It was exciting. He gave me his phone number, and once a week I would give him a call, go to his apartment and he would suck my cock. He did it with such relish, the way Stan had. Then I met another guy in the park and the same pattern developed."

"How did you feel about what you were doing?"

"Rotten, because I was sure that I must be a homosexual. There was no other way to look at it. Every book on the subject, every expert said that if a man engaged in homosexual acts, no matter how much heterosexual sex he enjoyed, he *was* homosexual."

"Did that stop you from doing it?"

"No, but it limited my enjoyment. The desire was too great to stop. I really loved it. But I hated being homosexual. A closet queen. I didn't feel homosexual. As a matter of fact, I didn't feel heterosexual. I felt sexual. I wanted sex and I wanted *all* I wanted. It relaxed me. Made me feel better. I now realize that of course I was attracted to men and women from the beginning. Even in camp as a kid during the circle jerks I wanted the other boys, and I wanted them to want me. Of course I never admitted it."

"When did you admit it for the first time?"

"I went into therapy. Thank God I got a doctor who did not see my homosexuality as a problem."

"Did he see any problem at all?"

"Yes. He was the first person to suggest to me that I might have a problem understanding what kind of sexual being I am."

"What kind is that?"

"Bisexual."

"How long did it take you to absorb that possibility?"

"Years. When I started to do more than just respond with men, I began to see that I wanted *them* as well as the sex. I met this guy and went to his place and found myself sucking him while he was sucking me, and that was the beginning–basic and limited but a beginning. And Freud aside, I think also that sex with men is more easily attainable, and that's part of the lure. Casual sex with a strange woman is hard to come by, and in my case, as I've explained, if I do come across it I have that intimacy bridge to cross. But I would say that by the time I was forty I had accepted myself as a bisexual."

We were at his apartment when he answered the last question, and he slumped down into an easy chair and sighed. "It didn't really take, though, until very recently. If it weren't for the women's movement and the gay lib explosion, I don't think I would really believe it even now, despite my doctor. You see, with my knowledge of psychology and my built-in respect for those who practiced it, I found it difficult to go up against the majority opinion. I suppose I really believed my doctor was telling me what I wanted to hear. Everything is how you look at it, after all."

"How did the women's movement affect your sexual attitudes toward yourself."

"'Options' is the first word that comes to my mind. The idea of permanent roles. It seemed to me that women were questioning that premise and that naturally appealed to me. I'd learned through my bisexual activity that I could play many roles, both active and passive, and they were all me. Aspects of me. I wasn't just an aggressive and assertive man who, however gentle, makes love to a woman who will eventually give way and become the passive recipient of my superman. Not that I don't enjoy that role. I do. But I also like being taken, being the passive one. It depends on the situation and the people involved. The possibilities of sexual interaction with other people is so much wider for the bisexual."

"How extensive is your sexual activity with men?"

"A few years ago I became aware of the gay underground, what's called a subculture. Actually it's a chic term to explain what is really middle-class tolerance of a way of life. I like sex. I meet men in the streets and there is still the park and on occasion I go to the baths. Then there are the bars. It's everywhere, really. The possibility of adventure is around every corner."

"Do you have any steady male lovers?"

"I have steady male contacts sexually. There have been men I maybe could have loved. A couple of years ago, in fact, I would say I did love a man, John. But people, male or female, make demands in a situation like that, and being married, I can't meet them."

"What do you mean by that?"

"Well, for instance, someone wants me to stay overnight. I just can't cut that. What would I say to Alice?"

"Does Alice know you are a bisexual?"

"No."

"Are you sure?"

"No, I'm not."

"Do you and Alice talk about sex?"

"We talk about everything. But when people have a marriage that's lasted thirty years, I think you have to have had areas private to each person. It doesn't matter what it is. But you have to have something of your own private to you."

"What does Alice have?"

"I don't know. She has something, though; otherwise she couldn't have kept me so intensely interested all these years."

"Would you like to know what it is?"

"I would and I wouldn't."

"What do you think is missing in your life sexually?"

"I have a fantasy. I meet a lovely woman alone on a stretch of beach or at a party. She's in her late thirties, intelligent, sexy, and we like each other from the start. I'm impotent the first time, but we get it on after that and we have a beautiful time."

"An affair?"

"An affair."

"How does it work out?"

"You mean how does it end? Sadly, but we're both, as they say, richer for the experience."

"Do you have such fantasies about meeting a man in that sense?"

"Yes, but only in a passing way. Men are so available that one's fantasy life isn't as extensive. Doesn't have to be."

"If you were forced to choose between homosexual and hetero-sexual life, which would you choose?"

"Neither. That's like asking a person with mixed parentage to choose and be either, say, Italian or Jewish. That person is both. To choose to be one or the other is possible in the sense that choice is possible. But no matter what you choose you're still going to be Italian and Jewish. I'm bisexual."

Like all of us, Harold G. lives *in* this world, and, like all of us, his psychosexual health is subject to whatever social pressure he en-counters. Until recently, despite a lifetime of consistent sexual con-tact with women, he believed himself to be a closet homosexual. As an intelligent, educated man he could not rationalize his homosexu-al activity away. He believed himself to be a secret homosexual because bisexuality, as all intelligent, educated people believed, did not exist. Only with the advent of various liberation movements was he able to see the possibility, as he puts it, of "options." If I had interviewed him before he achieved this new awareness, I would not have considered him a healthy bisexual. What makes him healthy is not only that he functions well in his work, that he is socially adept, that he is capable of deep intimacy with others over long periods of time, or even that he is relatively happy. All those things would not be enough if he still believed himself to be a closet homosexual, because there is too much inner conflict in such a belief to allow anyone to be considered healthy. But, interestingly, he let his preconceptions go when he saw the bisexual truth of himself. False belief was imposed on him by a society intent on the "either-or" solution to complex personal situations. It's unfortunate that Harold had to reach his middle years before acquiring this knowledge. But better late than never. Much better.

Harold G. is not, of course, a perfect sexual being. No one is. He says that his oldest brother is locked into the gay life and therefore "desperate"; in some ways, of course, Harold is also locked into his life with Alice. Although it appears to be an excellent relationship, some of his fantasies and activities might be seen as having an edge of desperation. Also, while his impotence isn't a major stumbling block, it is there nonetheless and indicates some sexual conflict. But relative to his generation, he seems a healthy man, and as of recent-ly, a healthy bisexual.

Hazel C.

Hazel is a delight. That was my first impression when she showed up at a Bisexual Forum discussion group some time ago. My initial impression has been strengthened since. I have gotten to know her well through her frequent attendance at the Forum and the one formal interview she agreed to tape.

Hazel, who is 29, shares a Greenwich Village high-rise apartment with Larry, who is 33. When I had asked her whether or not she lived alone, she said:

"I was taking an evening accounting class at N.Y.U. and needed a tutor. Larry helped me get an A-minus in the course. We began going together and after six months we took this great apartment. That was two years ago."

"Have you been seeing anyone else at the same time?"

"No. At least not for the last eighteen months. He satisfies me in so many ways that I have no desire to see others–men or women."

"I gather that your relationship with him is good. What are your future plans for the two of you?"

"My fantasy is to stay with Larry for the rest of my life. We are thinking of marriage, but we both need more time. I want to be sure, and he takes a long time accepting responsibility. But when he does he does. Then there is the question of my being black and his being white, though *we're* both cool about it."

"Do you want children?"

"Yes, both of us do. If we do get married I want to bring my Richie up from Baton Rouge and have him finally live with me."

At the age of 16 Hazel had given birth to a son, Richie. She had been seeing the father, Bill, for over two years. Although she didn't want to marry him, she continued to see him until she left Louisiana when she was 18.

"Was Bill the first man you ever had sex with?" I asked.

"Yes. At fourteen I started to play around with Bill. He taught me a lot. He made me feel comfortable about sex. Most of my sexual life and dealing with men I learned from him. I liked him a lot but we both saw other people at the same time. Even when Richie was born, I knew I didn't want to be tied down to him. What is more, I didn't want to be in Baton Rouge."

"Why?"

"My mother. I had to get away from her. She has this conservative religious outlook and a domineering way of expressing it. She just got all over me. Never let up. She's so cautious about everything. So in 1966 I just had had it. Really had it. So I picked up and came to New York. My older sister was a big help. She, with my mother's help, brought Richie up. He's thirteen now. A real big boy. My sister did a good job. I mean he's well behaved, full of fun. He laughs a lot. Last Christmas we spent a lot of nice time together. We talked about his coming to live with me. I want that so much."

"What did you do when you arrived in New York?"

"Well, I had enough money for, say, a month, so right away I found this sleep-in servant job in New Rochelle. You can imagine how I loved that, after leaving home to get away from taking orders. Anyway, my second day here I met this guy. He was ten years older. We moved in together after three months and then we had three months together before we had this real bad scene. He held on too tight. I was 'his woman' and all of that stuff. I couldn't believe it. It was like living at home again. I couldn't move. I couldn't talk to anyone. *Anyone*. He was insanely jealous. One night when he was away, I packed my stuff and moved out. I stayed with a friend who had a studio."

"What jobs have you held here?"

"I've had about eight jobs in these past eleven years. All kinds. But the jobs got better. Babysitter, receptionist, gal Friday, secretary. Now I'm executive secretary to the president of a corporation. I like it. The business is medium-sized so I'm not lost in it like a number. I'm a person there."

"How many men have you been with since you began going out?"

Spreading her hands as wide as her smile, she said, "A lot. Probably close to a hundred. I find it easy to meet men. They find me attractive and make the first move. Since I'm not shy, I also approach men, that is if I'm interested."

"Have all the relationships been short ones?"

"Most have except the three important ones, the three men I've loved and love. Larry, the one I'm living with. Bill in Baton Rouge. And Craig. I followed Craig out to California for a year when his company transferred him. I lived four years with him."

"Were you monogamous with Craig?"

"We both were for the first three years. He was bisexual and I was only the third woman he'd ever had. But we got along well. He had men from time to time that last year. In fact, he introduced me to Jane, the first woman I ever made love with."

"How many women have you been with since Jane?"

She took a sip of her Coke and curled her legs up on the sofa. "Let's see. I met Jane in 1974 and one year later we made it. We only had sex two times in all before I came back to New York. In New York I made love with two other women before I met Larry. So altogether there have been three women and four lesbian experiences."

"Are you physically attracted to women?"

"Yes. Some women turn me on just seeing them walk down the street. Especially their breasts–a low décolleté showing big boobs is a real turn-on. Also women's thighs."

"Do you enjoy sex more with a woman or with a man?"

"With men. Women aren't as satisfying for me. I guess it's because I enjoy heavy penetration of the vagina with a strong intensity. Jane used her fingers, but it wasn't as satisfying as a penis. But with women I enjoy touching and feeling flesh, especially breasts. I like caressing and sucking. I also like to kiss. In fact, I'm pretty active with both men and women in bed. I like doing the work and being on top although I enjoy different positions, too, like being on my hands and knees and getting it from the back."

"How often do you have sex?"

She smiled. "It depends on Larry's mood. Mine as well, I guess, but on the average four or five times a week. We both dig sex and each other."

"When did you first consider yourself bisexual?"

"In California with Craig. We saw a lot of gays and lesbians there. I had always considered myself straight. But then I had to work out in my head the role of the lesbian. I didn't want to scare off women, especially Jane, to whom I was strongly attracted. It became clear when I realized that I'm bisexual. That's how I allowed myself to make it with Jane the first time."

"Where on the Kinsey scale do you think you belong?" (See page 15 for an explanation of the Kinsey hetero/homosexual scale.)

"Philosophically I'm smack in the middle–a 'four,' fifty-fifty. Though my experience is much more with men, I'm open to women just as much. If Larry and I ever split up, I think I could love and live with a woman. In fact, my therapist's remark a number of years ago had a very strong influence on me. He once said that when you want to give or get love, it makes no difference which sex you get it from."

"How long have you been in therapy? Why did you begin it?"

"I've been going off and on since 1972. I've been in a group now for the last year and a half. I began because I started to have crying fits and didn't know why. My friend who was in therapy herself told me I should get help, and I did. I saw a Sullivanian who really helped me get in touch with my feelings–especially my bottled-up anger toward my mother and toward my boss at that time, who laid down some pretty strict rules at work. It was an excellent move, going into therapy. My relationships improved. Everything."

"Do you consider yourself healthy?"

She smiled, paused, and said, "If you had asked me that in 1972 I would have answered that I'm at least somewhat neurotic. But today if we use a health scale of say one to ten, I would say I'm nine, near the top on the healthy side."

"Who in your life knows about your bisexuality?"

"Larry does, of course. My best girl friend, who's also bi. All my other gay and bi friends. Some of my straight friends, though my two closest ones don't. Only my brother Phil in my family knows. Actually I told him this year. He was being hassled at school about the whole issue, although he hasn't had any homosexual experience, and in the discussion it just naturally came up. In fact, he was surprised to hear that in New York there are people who don't badmouth you for being gay or bisexual. In Louisiana everyone does, according to Phil, and I can believe it."

"Have you found that being black affects this aspect of your life?"

"Of course. Specifically I've found that I have trouble with a lot of black men. I shy away from them, though some of them turn me on very much. But they're so macho and their motto is 'You're a woman and I've got something for you!' I don't need *that* bullshit."

"One last question. Why, if you're seeing no one but Larry, do you come almost every week to the Bi-Forum discussions?"

She spoke without hesitation. "I'm able to express myself openly there to both men and women on an emotional level. I'm able to talk straight about my gay side as well as not having to downplay my relationship to men in general and with Larry in particular. I'm comfortable, open, and I know that people there understand and that it's okay to feel and be the way I am. . . ."

Hazel is open and relatively comfortable with herself. In her interactions with people at the meetings she is inwardly secure, supportive of others, and gives off warm feelings toward other people and about life in general. She has grown psychologically in the last ten years and is open to more positive change and growth in the future. She is liked by many and loved by her special friends. A healthy bisexual. A lovely woman.

Jane O.

Jane O. is not a patient of mine, but she has shared with me in four formal interviews her fantasies and her sexual history. She is an attractive woman of 38, a bit on the plump side. The plumpness suits her; it complements an open, generous nature. She married early, at 17, had several affairs while married, and was divorced after 20 years.

"You're from San Francisco originally?" I asked.

"Yes, my father worked for one of the large multinational corporations. When I was twelve, he was made vice-president in charge of everything and we all moved to New York."

"All?"

"Yes. My father, mother, two brothers and myself."

"Was it a happy move?"

"I didn't mind it. I liked the east. I liked New York. My father was a 'big deal' in the business world and as his daughter I benefited socially. I didn't have it bad at all. My brothers suffered the most."

"How?"

"They were my father's hope for immortality, and he really played the patriarch with them. He always had to be in control, and he controlled his sons with an iron hand. Because I was a girl, he left me more or less alone, and although I hated him for it at the time, I now realize that as a girl I was free to be myself. My mother is a nice but rather dull and passive woman. Anyway, I married early to get away from both of them and from what my father was doing to my brothers."

"Were you the youngest?"

"No. I'm two years younger than my brother Walt and four years older than Andrew."

"How do you get along with them now?"

"Walt and I are very close. Andrew works for my father, who is now executive vice-president."

"So you and Walt got away?"

"Yes. Walt is an engineer up in Boston. He never contacts anyone in the family except me. He's okay. A bisexual too, by the way."

"What about Andrew?"

"Straight and narrow like Father."

"So you married early?"

"Yes. I was seventeen. Sort of young, delicious, and rich. He was twenty-five, just out of law school, brilliant, good family, Father approved and I did love him. His name was, still is, Joe."

"What about college?"

"Well, I did go one year to Columbia, but the baby came and I dropped out to be a mother. I enjoyed being a mother. I have no regrets about that. Would you believe I'm a grandmother?" She showed me a picture of her six-month-old grandson, sitting in a highchair, his parents on either side. "That's my son and that's his wife. I have another son, unmarried. He's in college."

"How do they feel about the divorce?" I asked, handing back the picture.

"Well, not bad. What's hard on them, I think, is that I'm living with a woman now. That really came from left field. I don't think they believe it. But then I don't think children can ever believe their parents have sex of any kind. I had a wonderful sex life with their father. I'm sure I could climb into bed with him right now and enjoy it, although I wouldn't."

"Why did you leave him?"

"Leave *him*," she laughed. "Joe left me. You see, it was never a good marriage." She paused, shaking her head. "That's not entirely true. We were good parents and we did love each other at least for the first, say, eight to ten years, but we were trapped. Love isn't enough. Sex isn't enough. There has to be"–she brought her palms together, delicately pressing her fingertips–"there has to be closeness, intimacy, warmth, understanding. Closeness." Her fingers bent and closed. "Closeness. Do you know what I mean? Joe and I had everything but intimacy. He was and is a very busy and successful man. He's a public man, if you understand what I'm saying. He's got this need to reach as many people as possible. Joe is a politician, really. Me, I like one person at a time. Or a family. If things are okay between me and one other person, I'm fine. Joe has to be okay with the world. Closeness with one person scares him. So over the years I kept pushing him to intimacy, and finally it reached the point where he had to either love me or leave me and, being Joe, he left.

"Walked out the door one day and it was over. He married his secretary, if you can believe it. Pretty young girl. Hell, I don't blame him. He could never be for me what I needed. I was hurt at first. Bone hurt, you know, but then I began to realize something. I was free. The children were grown, my husband was gone, and, goddamn it, I was free to have a look and see if I couldn't maybe find what I was looking for and could never get from Joe. I used to have these fantasies while I was married about other people. That's what led to the affairs, all with men. They didn't amount to much really. Just bored housewife filling an afternoon kind of thing."

"Do you want to talk about them?"

"Not really."

"Do you think they are pertinent to your bisexuality?"

"I guess anything sexual is pertinent in this conversation. Let's see, what can I tell you? There were four men over a twenty-year period. When I look back on it now, it seems that all the sex was in cars, movie houses, motels. Sex on the run. Sometimes it was satisfying, sometimes it wasn't, but it filled or killed time. Once I actually picked up a man in Grand Central Station. We met after that for two years, every couple of weeks. He was killing time too. . . ."

"Did you like, or love, any of these men?"

"I'll never know, because my love . . . my loyalty was for Joe. I thought that eventually Joe and I would find each other so I never really gave enough of myself to love the other men, although I certainly liked them."

"Was Joe having affairs?"

"I'm sure he must have, and of course he certainly did with his secretary."

"Why did you choose sex as a way of killing time?"

"Oh, sex was only one way. I played tennis, redecorated the house in the country every six months, traveled, wrote poetry—that wasn't killing time. Sex was just one way. Sex with men, that is. Men sort of demand it, so if you want to spend time with a man outside of your marriage, sex is the handle. Often *I* could have just gone for a long drive and talked. Just been with him, but that's harder to justify than sex. I think. I don't really know. What I do know is that it wasn't that way with women."

"Your bisexual life began during your marriage?"

"I didn't think of it as a bisexual life exactly. But yes, it did. After fifteen years into the marriage."

"Do you remember a specific incident or did it grow in your fantasy life first?"

"That's hard to say. Four years before the divorce I went on a weekend with this woman I'd known in college. We hadn't seen each other in years. We took a fall drive up into Vermont to the Canadian border, stopping at little inns and just having a close, warm time. We were closer than we had ever been before. I think the weather and time of year had something to do with it. The leaves were turning, and each day was what we kept calling 'Pumpkin Perfect.' We talked and talked and went on hikes and laughed . . . *how* we laughed. At an inn in Woodstock, Vermont, two attractive men asked us to dinner. We liked them, but we politely turned down the invitation. Later we wondered why. I mean, they were attractive, intelligent men."

"What did you conclude?"

"We didn't want to dilute what we were having. We didn't want to lose each other in some competitive game with the opposite sex."

"Would that have been necessary?"

"Not necessary, but it usually happens between men and women. I mean, there's the pairing, and then there's dealing with who's going to get whom. Usually the men decide, and before it's over you've lost your friend to some one-night-stand lover. When I think of all the times I've sold out my friend for the momentary attention of some man and all the times I've been sold out."

"All is fair in love and war?"

"Exactly. And it's awful. Men sell each other out for women too. It shouldn't happen."

"Did you and your friend become lovers?"

"Oh no. Nothing happened, but I wanted something to happen. When I got back home–she lives in Texas–I thought about her. One afternoon I was thinking about her hands, of all things. She has lovely hands, and I found myself masturbating and thinking about her. Whenever I masturbated before, it was because Joe was out of town on business, and then I would think of men but in a vague sort of way. I would imagine some man having me on my kitchen floor or behind a machine at the laundromat. Crazy things like that. But with her, I would think of us in bed just loving and touching and kissing for hours. It was delicious. Well, we never did have each other. Never saw her again as a matter of fact.

"About six months later, though, Joe was away and I met this woman at the Museum of Modern Art. We shared a table at the cafeteria. We just hit it off so nicely. We made a date for lunch the following week. She took me to her apartment, and, no kidding, within ten minutes we were on the bed and oh my."

"That was your first sexual experience with a woman?"

"Yes."

"What did you feel?"

"Good. I felt good. I felt a new part of myself. God, it was glorious."

"Did it last?"

"No. She moved to North Carolina. That was all for a while. After the divorce I met a man I liked tremendously, an account executive for one of the big ad agencies. He was a sweet man, very sexy and considerate. He put the word out and I got a job in an art gallery. For about three or four months it was really intense but heavy because he was married. I had no desire to hurt another woman the way I had been hurt, so after lots of emotional ripping and tearing I broke it off. It was hard because I really liked him, but you have to be careful or you go from the frying pan into the fire. More than finding a lover I wanted to find myself, which for me means finding the *right* lover. Then one quiet afternoon a young girl came into the gallery. She was about twenty-four and we got into an interesting conversation. We made a date for dinner and we had a nice thing for a while."

"Sex?"

"Oh yes."

"How was it?"

"Good, but another filler. It had everything but *it*, if you know what I mean. That closeness just wasn't there."

"Did you have the closeness with the ad man?"

"Yes. Very much so. That's what made it so hard to let him go."

"So you kept seeing the young girl."

"Yes, and then through her I met Sue. We were at a *vernissage* and . . . well, within a few weeks I was in love. I fell in love with Sue the way I did with Joe years ago. All the way."

"Does Sue have much in common with Joe?"

"No. Nothing. She's as different as a man is from a woman. I don't know why we love each other but we do. It may be the best relationship I've ever had."

"Do you still have fantasies about men?"

"Sure. Depends on where my head is at that moment, though I really masturbate very little these days. I guess I'm into the lesbian life now. I go off on weekends with Sue and other women. We share a house in the Hamptons in summer. It's nice. I have a lot of lesbian friends. There is a feeling of comradeship between six or eight of us that is new and wonderful."

"Had you any inkling ten years ago that you would be doing what you are doing now?"

"Oh, lord no," she laughed. "Isn't life amazing? It just never lets up."

"Do you consider yourself homosexual now?"

"Not really. I don't like the label."

"Do you consider yourself heterosexual?"

"I don't like that label either. I guess I'm most comfortable thinking of myself as bi, but that's a label too, isn't it? Well, listen, does it really matter? I've loved both men and women in my life. I'm a lover. Let's just call me a lover. Is that fair?. . ."

Indeed it is. Jane O. has shown a capacity to love both men and women and enjoy sex with both. This is not to say that she doesn't have some neurotic patterns that show through in some of her comments–for example, she glossed over her relationship of 20 years with Joe, which raises questions; and there is more pain behind her "bored housewife kind of thing" remark than she showed. But had she not turned to women for love, everyone would probably agree on her healthy ability to get into a new meaningful relationship. She is not "pathological," though, for doing so. There are many possible reasons or motives for such a decision, but whatever they are, if a person shows the ability to find meaning, deep intimacy, and happiness in his or her relationships, that person surely deserves to be considered psychosexually healthy.

PART III:
THE BISEXUAL IN SOCIETY

Chapter 8

Sociological Findings

Sociology is the study of human beings in groups, in communities of all kinds–mainstream or marginal, privileged or oppressed, "above-ground" or "underground." On the level of sexuality, homosexuals and heterosexuals constitute such communities. They overlap in professional and family life, but sexually at least, the lines of demarcation are clear. But why should this be so?

"Good fences make good neighbors," Robert Frost's farmer advises. But Frost questions that. *Why* do good fences make good neighbors? He gets no answer from the farmer, who is not speaking out of wisdom but out of fear.

Male and female homosexuals have formed their own communities because no room was made for them in the mainstream. They couldn't join fully in the mainstream without loss of personal identity as men, as women–as human beings. They renamed themselves "gay" and "lesbian," which they preferred to the straight world's labels of "queer" and "dyke" (though some of course have since defiantly readopted those terms).

A male operating freely in both homosexual and the heterosexual world can choose to define himself as bisexual and not need to form or join his own subculture. He doesn't need the fence. He can live in both communities, moving back and forth as his needs or desires dictate. Although he may decide to hide his "queerness" from the straights and his "closet behavior" from the gays, he does not necessarily need to belong to a community of bisexuals. He is among his kind when he is among *human beings*.

This is not to say that a need for a bisexual community doesn't exist at all. It does. But not for the same reasons the male and female homosexuals created their subculture. Men and women gather together into groups primarily for mutual protection and support. The bisexual can survive in either the heterosexual or homosexual camp, or both, and that makes him or her an elusive subject for the sociologist. If there were such a thing as a bisexual community, there would doubtless not be as few sociological studies as there are.

Philip W. Blumstein and Pepper Schwartz, of the Department of Sociology at the University of Washington, have done extensive sociological work on bisexuality, published in *Sexual Deviance and Sexual Deviants*. They report:

We know that a great many people have sexual relations with members of both sexes. Seldom do they claim to divide their attention and commitment absolutely equally (hence the misleading quality of the term bisexual), but both types of sexual experience have independent importance for them. Despite the documented existence of large numbers of such people, one is hard-pressed to find much systematic scientific literature on the topic of bisexuality. Psychoanalysis, for example, has already declared itself on this issue: it is irrelevant. Orthodox Freudian analysts feel that bisexuality does not exist as a clinical entity; a person is either heterosexual or homosexual. The person's expressed self-identification is of no consequence, except as a symptom of inability to come to grips with his or her true sexuality. Irving Bieber has stated: "I conceive of two distinct categories–heterosexual and homosexual. . . . The two categories are . . . mutually exclusive and cannot be placed on the same continuum. . . . A man is homosexual if his behavior is homosexual. Self-identification is not relevant. . . ."

The Lesbian community provides a perfect counterpoint. In it, claiming a bisexual identity receives no community validation, but rather a great deal of negative response. More important, it is precisely in this community that women learn how to "understand" their own sexuality, the motivations to attribute to themselves, and the boundaries of the sexually possible, the sexually likely, and the sexually impossible. In this context one learns that bisexuality is possible, but uncommon, and that bisexuality is really an inability to come to grips with "true" underlying Lesbianism.

So we see one reason why the bisexuals have not declared themselves in a community. The stigma of homosexual behavior in the heterosexual world and the equal intolerance for heterosexual behavior in the homosexual world have left most bisexuals feeling they have no choice but to pose as one or the other, in accordance with the values of whichever camp they are presently in. But the bisexual's need for community may be just as great as any one else's.

From 2 to 6 on the Klein Sexual Orientation Grid–that is, from heterosexual mostly (2) to gay/lesbian mostly (6)–the range of bisexual possibilities is so wide that heterosexuals and homosexuals often find it incomprehensible. What has helped open and widen this range of possibilities is a relaxation of sexual self-repression, hence, an increased openness and flexibility with regard to the gender of sexual partners on the part of bisexuals–both those whose major sexual focus is women and whose incidental focus is men, and those whose major sexual focus is men and whose incidental focus is women. Included somewhere with this range is the bisexual whose focus is nearly evenly divided between men and women, and the individual whose bisexuality is sequential–a person who, for example, has lived with a mate of one sex and after separation lives with a mate of the opposite sex.

Morton Hunt's *Sexual Behavior in the Seventies*, does not even mention bisexual behavior on the contents page or in the index. It is not exactly true to state that Hunt does not *consider* bisexual behavior. He does. But he calls it homosexual:

> Some self-styled bisexuals, as we have indicated, are basically homosexual but seek to minimize their conflicts and sense of deviance by having occasional heterosexual episodes.

There is the qualifier "some" at the beginning of the sentence, but Hunt follows with:

> Others have had a bisexual period when, for many reasons, they still thought or hoped that they were heterosexual, though they eventually recognized that their real orientation was toward same-sex partners.

These statements are misleading. They feed the nonexistence myth. What Hunt is describing are some of the bisexuals found on the KSOG at 5 or 6 (predominantly gay/lesbian). Of course, no mention is made of the "self-styled bisexual" who is basically heterosexual but seeks to minimize conflict by having occasional homosexual episodes (the 2 or 3 on the KSOG). The heterosexuality represented by many doctors and sociologists as the superior option is never considered as a possible source of personal conflict. I would suggest a reading or rereading of D. H. Lawrence's *Women in Love* as an example of a heterosexual conflict (see page 150). The conflict of the 2 or 3 may be different from that of the 5 and the 6–the 2 or the 3 is more likely to live in the heterosexual community–but it can be there nonetheless.

A moving illustration of this difference is the story told by a young Californian now residing (with his female friend of four years) in New York City. He is 26 and the young woman is 24. At a meeting of the Bisexual Forum, they were asked by the moderator whether they were bisexual. The woman shook her head no and the man lowered his eyes. He tried to speak but tears began to fill his eyes. The woman spoke for him at first. "We have been living together for four years and are very much in love. I can tell you without qualification that Sydney is a wonderful lover to me and that we have no problems in that area. He's ardent and loving and we are very happy together."

Then the woman looked at him. He'd recovered somewhat and began to speak for himself. "*I'm* bisexual. For the longest time I had these fantasies about getting emotionally and physically close to a male. I thought I must be really homosexual but I still liked women, especially Debbie. I mean I really love Debbie and I desire her in every way, so how could I be homosexual? My need to be close with a male never sidetracked me away from my real feelings and my fantasies when it came to women, but I had this other need and it was driving me crazy. I sat on it and sat on it until, I don't know, until I couldn't any more. Anyway I had this really close friend. We had been friends for about six years. So about a year ago I told him how I felt. I told him I wanted to . . . you know, get closer, and he ran . . . the friendship was over. He just didn't want to see me anymore, and I thought I must be some kind of monster because he really ran. I haven't seen him since and we were *really* close. So anyway I told Debbie. I had to tell someone. She was wonderful. She *is* wonderful. She said in time I would make another friendship. She was right. About three months ago I met this man and he came to dinner and we really hit it off. Only two weeks ago the same thing happened as with my friend, and this guy also took off. He hangs up when I call him on the phone. I was hurt, I felt guilty. I said to Debbie I must be a homosexual, and she said if anybody knew I wasn't a homosexual it was she. And then she said"–at this point he choked up once more–"I must be bisexual. And when she said it I knew it was true. It was just true. Anyway, that's why I'm here."

Research into bisexuality is hampered by three basic difficulties: the myth of nonexistence; the difficulty in interpreting sociological findings; the confusion of labels and identities, including the one of self-identity.

What are some of the sociological findings? What sort of population have we been describing? How many bisexuals are there? How many of those are active bisexuals, how many historical bisexuals? How many have had actual bisexual experiences and how many bisexual fantasies only?

In Chapter 2 we described Kevin and the difficulty in interpreting his statistics. As we saw on the seven variables of sexual orientation he turned out to be a: 6, 4, 7, 1, 4, 2, and 5 (see page 19). These numbers only describe Kevin at the present time. His past history and his ideal would most likely give us still different sexual orientation values.

To complicate matters even further, sociosexual studies of bisexuals are extremely difficult to obtain, and the interpretations of the results of those that are available are full of problems. Sampling methods and interviewing techniques yield different results even with the best of intentions–and even when done by brilliant researchers. And yet the studies are useful. When interpreted conservatively and wisely they can lead to knowledge and give us working bases. Let's set aside for the moment the problem of measuring the infinitely varied degrees and shifts of individual bisexual behavior, and look instead at the "bisexual community" in terms of overall numbers.

How many bisexuals are there? What percentage of the population is bisexual? There are a number of popular notions on this question. Some say there are no bisexuals at all (the nonexistence theory), others count fewer bisexuals than homosexuals, and still others believe everyone is bisexual. Actually, around 15 percent of the male population is definable on the Kinsey scale as bisexual if we look at a three-year period in the lives of his respondents; and half that percentage of the female population, i.e., 7-8 percent. This means that, conservatively speaking, there are 25-30 million bisexuals in the U.S.A. A detailed look at these figures can be seen in Note 1 at the end of the chapter, page 128.

In 1993, John Billy et al. found in a survey of over 3,300 men between the ages of 20 and 39 that 2.3 percent of the men had engaged in same-gender sexual activity during the last ten years and that 1 percent reported being exclusively homosexual during this interval. This is much lower than what Kinsey found and is somewhat lower than some of the recent studies conducted in Britain, France, and Denmark which found that between 3 and 4 percent of men had had a homosexual partner at one time.

The figures support the finding that there are more bisexuals than homosexuals–between twice and eleven times as many, depending on who is counting and how (see Note 2, p. 130). Whatever the exact figure, in my view it is extremely large–probably between five and ten times as many bisexuals as homosexuals.

Note 3, p. 130, describes studies suggesting that 50 percent of "homosexual" males and over 75 percent of "homosexual" females have had sexual experiences with members of both genders.

A bisexual who relates on an emotional and sexual plane to both men and women would, in many if not most cases, desire to and actually enter into marriage. On the number of married people who are bisexual, the figures vary between 2 and 10 percent of presently married people, with men carrying a higher percentage than women. Of those separated and divorced, the percentages that are bisexual approach the total percentages of men and women that are bisexual (see Note 4, p. 131).

The married bisexual who wishes to remain monogamous must refrain only from extramarital relations with the other gender, but with the same gender as well. Does the bisexual actually do that?

Does he or she practice fidelity as often as the married heterosexual? One myth about bisexuals holds that they share the sexual bed indiscriminately and often with others of the same sex. Exact statistics are not available, but in general one can say that bisexual men and women probably do have more extramarital affairs than their heterosexual counterparts. For the population as a whole the figures show that 50 percent of all men and 20 percent of all women have at some time during their marriage had sexual relationships on the outside. From my experience the figures for bisexuals are definitely higher. The married bisexual man who has outside homosexual contacts is relatively common. The married woman who has an affair with another woman is not quite as common though in a non-random sample, Janet Bode's study, *View from Another Closet*, found that only 33 percent of the women surveyed admitted to monogamous serial relationships.

Hunt found that only 20 percent of the spouses of those who had extramarital relations in the general population knew of their partner's outside affairs. For bisexuals the figure would probably be lower if the spouse did not know at all of the partner's bisexual inclination, and higher if either the mate knew that fact or if both members of the marriage were bisexual.

However, I'd like to stress that by no means do all bisexuals feel the need to have sexual relations with both genders at any given time. Many homosexuals too, like many heterosexuals, are satisfied with one deep primary relationship. McWhirter and Mattison's survey of male homosexual couples found that some men had lived with women up to fifteen years before changing to male lovers. As a homosexual group, however, most of the men were openly non-monogamous.

In their survey of male homosexuals, Weinberg and Williams compared them to the bisexuals (6 and 7 vs. 3-5 on the Kinsey scale). They found that bisexuals were more involved with women sexually, were more likely to have been married, and, as might be expected, were less involved exclusively with homosexuals. Bisexuals concealed their homosexual component more than homosexuals and expected narrow discrimination from the heterosexual world. Weinberg and Williams found no data to support the thesis that bisexuals had more psychological problems.

Between 1973 and 1975 Drs. Blumstein and Schwartz interviewed 150 bisexual men and women to study bisexual behavior and identity. Their most consistent finding on both sexes showed that there was "little coherent relationship between the amount and 'mix' of homosexual and heterosexual behavior in a person's biography and that person's choice to label himself or herself as bisexual, homosexual, or heterosexual." People with little or no homosexual experience sometimes identified themselves as bisexual, while others with considerable bisexual activity labeled themselves as heterosexual or homosexual.

Not unexpectedly, female bisexuals were found to be more romantic than male bisexuals. When involved with another woman, females labeled themselves lesbian; when involved with a man, heterosexual. When unattached, they would frequently label themselves bisexual. Males more often continuously identified themselves as bisexual.

Another important if not surprising conclusion of Blumstein and Schwartz's study was the changeability in sexual object choices. Significant experience with one gender did not necessarily determine future sexual orientation. Bisexuals came to their present state of functioning from extremely varied backgrounds: some early, some late, some changing suddenly, others undergoing a gradual transition over decades.

It was also found that both the heterosexual and homosexual communities generally viewed the bisexual in a negative light. The heterosexual world looked upon the bisexual as a homosexual, while the homosexual subcultures viewed the bisexual as someone just going through a phase; they defined the bisexual's identity as not real (in other words, nonexistent). Two exceptions were found in the heterosexual world. The libertarian element of the population viewed bisexuality more liberally . . . the bisexuals "did their own thing." The women's liberation and the smaller men's liberation movements, devoted and finely attuned to the political and emotional needs of their own gender, were in sympathy at least with the idea–if not the reality–of bisexuality.

Charlotte Wolff studied 150 British bisexual men and women. In 1977 she published her findings in her book, *Bisexuality, A Study*. Some of the major findings were that: (1) the males in her sample had significantly more homosexual lovers, while the females had significantly more heterosexual lovers; (2) though the men and women reported no differences in their numbers of casual heterosexual sex encounters, the males had significantly more frequent casual homosexual encounters; and (3) though the majority of bisexuals felt that bisexuality was a social disadvantage, they nevertheless thought it to offer emotional, mental, and creative advantages.

In 1985 Regina Reinhardt found in a study of 26 bisexual women in heterosexual relationships, that the couples maintained satisfactory relationships. Half of the women were maintaining sexual relationships with other women. They had 1.5 sexual contacts per month with their female partners while having sex 3 times per week with their male partners.

In 1991, as part of a larger study on AIDS in the Netherlands, van Zessen and Sandford interviewed 1001 Dutch people with respect to their sexual orientation. Their findings showed that while only 1.1% had had bisexual experiences in the preceding year, 7.8% labeled themselves as neither exclusively heterosexual nor exclusively homosexual. This figure is nevertheless quite a bit lower than the American statistics mentioned above.

A rather complete literature review on research on the size of the bisexual population, commissioned by the Global Program on AIDS of the World Health Organization, was put together in 1990 by Boulton and Weatherburn in the United Kingdom. It found that due to different definitions of bisexuality and the different populations studied, the results varied from a low percentage similar to that found in the Dutch study quoted above to as high as the Kinsey study done so many years ago. All one can say in summary is that accurately determining the size of the bisexual population is extremely difficult because (1) it is further subdivided into various distinct groups (for example, self-identified bisexuals, closeted 'heterosexuals,' married men), (2) there seem to be as many definitions of bisexuality as there are research studies, and (3) different cultures view the bisexual in completely different ways.

In 1991, Rob A. P. Tielman edited a book on the findings of bisexuality and its relation to HIV/AIDS as found in many countries throughout the world.

Two books that portray the life stories of bisexuals themselves have recently been published. In 1988, *Bisexual Lives* (edited by the Off Pink Collective) was published in England; and in 1991, *Bi Any Other Name: Bisexual People Speak Out* (edited by Loraine Hutchins and Lani Kaahumanu) was published by Alyson Publications, Inc.

In 1991, Amity Pierce Buxton published *The Other Side of the Closet*, giving the results of a study of hundreds of marriages where one of the partners was gay or bisexual. The book explores the major issues straight spouses confront when their partners declare their homosexuality or bisexuality.

In 1993, Ron Fox completed his study of 835 self-defined bisexuals using a lengthy questionnaire regarding self-disclosure and sexual orientation. His results showed that the greatest number of disclosures were made to friends and relationship partners and to helping professionals.

The 1983-88 studies by Martin Weinberg et al. of close to 800 bisexually indentified individuals is being published in 1994 by Oxford University Press. These studies investigated the characteristics of persons who adopt a bisexual identity as well as give the effect of AIDS on sexual preference.

The social disadvantages of being bisexual are many, as they are for any group living without full recognition and rights. The bisexual, however, because he or she does not live in community, does not suffer the burden of sole identification with any one group, and this of course is often an advantage. For example, the bisexual who chooses to identify with the homosexual community need never be made aware of the sociological problems inherent in his or her bisexuality. He or she also need not deal with the problems of being exclusively homosexual. Despite where they live, they can have, if they choose, a foot in the other camp. This may still cause the individual conflict and pain, even though it is usually blamed on matters having nothing to do with being bisexual.

In the case, for example, of the reasonably happily married man who sleeps from time to time with men, the primary problem is often not seen as bisexuality, but as infidelity or homosexuality–the man's wife, if she finds out, is probably going to be upset first because her husband has been "unfaithful" and second because he is "homosexual." This couple may take their problem out of the home and into psychotherapy or marriage counseling without the condition of bisexuality ever being mentioned. If the couple should turn to the church for counsel, the man will almost surely never be advised to atone for the "sin of bisexuality." His sins will most likely be identified as the sins of adultery and homosexuality.

The bisexual has simply been sociologically nonexistent–the church, the state, and, to a certain extent, science can't find him or her. What's needed, it would seem, to end this peculiar limbo state is a valid sense of identity, of community.

It's difficult to say what will create this. Perhaps the acute sense of isolation common to many bisexuals, especially those who are married, will be a contributing factor. Married bisexuals–such as the man described above–live for the most part with one basic social fear: the discovery of the homosexual component in their natures. They isolate themselves from the homosexual community on a social level while often feeling isolated in the heterosexual community in which they live. They know that if their inclinations are discovered, not only will they be labeled homosexual but their marriages will be seen as a cover-up.

"Marriage as a cover-up" may be true in some bisexual cases, but only a minority. Bisexuals who stray from their marriage beds to sleep with someone of the same sex don't necessarily lose sexual interest in their spouses, just as married heterosexual men or women who sleep with others don't necessarily lose interest in their mates. Some homosexual men do marry to prove they are straight when they are not; but 70 percent of homosexuals in the survey by Saghir and Robins (*Male & Female Homosexuality*) said that they would not consider resorting to marriage as a cover-up, and 83 percent said they would not consider marriage with a lesbian as a cover-up. Most of the married bisexuals had not married to hide a homosexual component. They married because life and sex with a member of the opposite gender had definite appeal.

There are also married bisexuals who are monogamous and would no more "cheat" on their husbands and wives than would heterosexual men and women who hold the same values. If a woman lives in marriage for 20 years with one man, never straying from his bed, is she, one may ask, in any way describable as bisexual? Yes–if, before the marriage, she engaged in sex with a woman;

or during the marriage her sexual fantasies, either masturbatory or during intercourse, had homosexual aspects; or if after her marriage she finds another mate, who this time is a woman, as was the case of Jane O., described in Chapter 7.

In marriage, though, it is the man who is generally more open to explore bisexuality. With the women's movement and the diminishing "double standard," this dichotomy is growing less clear-cut, but the fact is that men–homosexual, heterosexual, and bisexual–are still more able to openly express their need for sexual fulfillment. And because of this, sex with males is much more easily available than with females. If a heterosexual married male on a business trip to a strange city wants sexual contact, he will more often than not have to pay for it. If a bisexual male on a business trip in a strange city wants sexual contact with a male, he can have it literally within minutes in gay bars or baths for the price of a drink or small entrance fee. In some cities he can go to the parks or other "cruising" spots and have sex without spending a dime (although this "exploitation" of homosexual availability by bisexuals is resented in the gay community).

The lack of a bisexual subculture is being felt, although those who feel it most aren't always sure of exactly what it is they feel. Words such as "longing," "diffused," "something missing," and "when in Rome" are used by bisexuals, both male and female, to describe their feelings. One of the most telling remarks was made by a young man at a meeting of the Bisexual Forum in New York City. As guest speaker I asked the group, "Do you as bisexuals feel the lack of a bisexual subculture?"

The question seemed to confuse them. Their silence made me realize that the question I had asked was more loaded than I thought.

"What do you mean by 'subculture'?" a young man finally asked. "You mean like a bar or something? What for? If you want a woman for companionship, you go to a straight singles bar. And if the night is long and you want a man, you go to a gay bar. What would a bisexual bar mean?"

"I don't think a bar is a good example," a woman said. "I don't go to bars."

"Well, suppose you did," the young man responded. "Would

you need a bisexual bar to find what you want, or a bisexual country club or church? What for?"

"I suppose you're right," she answered, "but I don't know."

"Do *you* feel the lack of a subculture?" I asked her.

"I don't know. I'm sorry to keep saying that, but I do know that if I wanted companionship for an evening, it might be nice to go someplace and meet men and women where I could be open and myself. I mean, I might not necessarily want a *man* or a *woman*. I might want to meet a person. It would be nice to go out with the idea of meeting someone without thinking it has to be of one gender or the other. There are times when I *want* a man or *want* a woman, but that may be because I have no other option. It may be that what I want is a nice human being to make love with. That at times for me could be a man or a woman. If there was a bisexual bar, say, I could go there without any preconceived idea of what I want. I might think I want a woman and then meet a really sweet man and want him. Now that I think of it, a bisexual bar or restaurant would be a place to go to find out *how* you feel by just being with men and women. People." She paused. "Just like here."

The woman's answer strikes me as going to the very heart of the bisexual problem. Bisexuals, though enjoying a wider possibility of choice in the pursuit of sexual love, must pursue those possibilities on grounds not necessarily of their choice. To find out who among bisexuals actually desire a bisexual community, and to explore the advantages and disadvantages of the lack of one as seen by bisexuals themselves, I surveyed a group of bisexual men and women in the late 1970s as part of an overall investigation into the bisexual in society. I handed out questionnaires to 150 people who showed up at the Bisexual Forum. I obtained an unusually high response; only six people did not wish to participate. Such a high response was helped by the support of Chuck Mishaan, founder of the Forum, who explained the purpose of the survey to everyone present. Study of bisexuals in their own group was not common in the late 1970s. At that time only in San Francisco (the Bi-Center), Santa Barbara, and Miami did other bisexual groups exist. The situation has changed and now in the early 1990s, there are about 50 bisexual organizations (most of them small, however) spread all over the United States. I will discuss the changes in the bisexual community

over the past 15 years in more detail in Chapter 10. Appendix B.,
p. 189 presents the detailed reactions of the 144 people at the
Bisexual Forum who responded. The major conclusions which I
still find to be valid in 1992 are discussed below.

Eighty-eight percent of those responding were bisexual to some
extent, and a great majority of these identified themselves as such.
(This contradicts the findings of Blumstein and Schwartz ["Bisexuality in Men," *Urban Life*] who found that the bisexual self-label
didn't correspond to actual experience or feelings.) Of those responding, 70 percent were male and 30 percent female. This discrepancy probably has less to do with bisexuality than with social events
in New York City, at which males very often outnumber females,
particularly at night. The average age of the women was 28.5 years,
of the men, 32.4 years. The education level was high, women having
a mean educational level of 15 years schooling and men 16 years. All
but three respondents had finished high school and many had mas-
ters' or doctorate degrees. The most frequent answer to the question
of occupation was "student" (around 10 percent). The occupations
of the other respondents ranged from driller to professor, musician to
housewife. In general the Forum seemed to attract a much larger
percentage of professionals than found in the general population.

Almost 60 percent were single; the remainder were divided among
the married and the previously married. Almost half lived alone; the
others lived with spouses, roommates, parents, lovers, children, relatives, or at school, in that order of frequency. On the question of
which parent they were closer to, the women were equally divided
between both parents, while over two-thirds of the men were closer
to their mothers. In our culture this isn't very surprising–I believe
these figures are representative of the population in general.

Self-labeling of the bisexuals corresponded closely with their
behavior. Over 75 percent of the respondents who put themselves
between 1 and 5 on the Kinsey scale (using Kinsey's original range
of 0 to 6) also considered themselves to be bisexual. The average
woman was 2.4 on the Kinsey scale, the average man a bit higher at
2.5, which indicates that the average person here was slightly more
heterosexual than homosexual on the continuum. Of those who
were exclusively heterosexual or homosexual, more than nine out
of ten were heterosexual. The close fit of behavior to identity

showed itself also in their responses to which gender they preferred sexually and to which gender they sexually fantasized about. Those who labeled themselves on the heterosexual end of the Kinsey scale (1 and 2) preferred and fantasized most often about the opposite sex. On the homosexual end of the scale the same gender was predominant in both preference and fantasy.

Interestingly, the bisexual label was adopted at a relatively late age. Of those who considered themselves bisexual, they first did so at an average age of 24. This held true for both men and women. A majority of members of both sexes were sexually attracted to the opposite sex before becoming aware of sexual attraction to their own sex. The women became aware of their heterosexual feelings at the average age of 11, while the men first realized theirs at an average age of 13. On the average, awareness of homosexual feelings began for women and men at the ages of 16 and 17 respectively. The difference between the sexes is pronounced when the ages of their initial homosexual activities are contrasted. While on the average the first heterosexual activity for both women and men was at the age of 16, the first homosexual experience for men was at 18, and the first for women at 23. Bode found that 20 percent of bisexual women had homosexual experience first before participating in heterosexual activity. Of our female respondents, 17 percent did so. On the other hand, 36 percent of the men in our study had a homosexual experience first. There is another point of interest regarding the age of first sexual activity. The average woman had her first heterosexual activity at the age of 15 1/2, while her first experience of penile-vaginal intercourse occurred two and one-half years later, at 18. For men the difference between first activity and first intercourse was less than two years–16 years old vs. 17 1/2 years.

How open are bisexuals about their sexual orientation? Seventy percent of the respondents' close friends, whose sexual orientation they knew, were heterosexual, 20 percent were homosexual, and only 10 percent were bisexual. In other words, the bisexuals moved primarily in the heterosexual world and considerably less in the homosexual world. Their association with other bisexuals was minimal. When the respondents listed the people in their lives who knew of their bisexuality, their responses suggested that the closet door was selectively open. For the majority, parents, siblings, relatives, and work associates were not privy to this information. On the other hand, almost half of the spouses knew of their orientation, and 62 percent had friends who did (with an average of over eight friends each who were in on it).

Where were the sexual partners of the bisexual respondents found? All over. Almost every conceivable place or situation was named by one or another of the respondents. However, for the women, only one source occurred with frequency: both heterosexual and homosexual contacts were made through friends. Men also used friends as contact sources but, with some degree of frequency, they also met women at parties, bars, and at work. Male homosexual contacts showed the greatest variance, with bar contacts accounting for a quarter of all places listed. Friends, parties, and baths were also mentioned more than a couple of times. Many different places and opportunities were used to meet others, with personal introductions through friends being the second most common, after male homosexual contacts at bars.

As we know, the bisexual is less repressed with respect to gender, being able to eroticize both sexes. But how does this influence other aspects of his and her sexual behavior? Does it lead the bisexual to have more lovers than do either heterosexuals or homosexuals? It would seem to. Though there were respondents who had only one partner over a long period of time, partners in general were relatively numerous. In the month prior to answering the questionnaire, the female bisexuals had on average 1.5 male partners and 0.7 female partners. The men had an average of 1.7 female partners and 2.4 male partners. During the previous year the female bisexuals had 4.7 heterosexual partners and 3.0 homosexual ones, while the male bisexuals had 9.2 different female partners and 12.9 male partners.

It's interesting that the bisexuals' rate of participation in sex with two or more people at the same time was higher than for the population in general. Hunt found that 40 percent of single males had had some sexual experience in the presence of more than one other person and 25 percent of single males had experienced multiple-partner sex. For females and married people the figures were significantly lower. Our questionnaire did not differentiate between the above two types of activity (sex *with* and sex *in the presence of* more than one other person). Sixty-three percent of the bisexuals had sex with two or more other people at the same time at least once in their lives. In the previous year, 46 percent of the respondents had had such an experience, while for the previous month it was 23 percent.

It's not easy to interpret such findings in the absence of additional relevant information. Were these multiple-partner experiences partner swapping, "swinging," or were they threesomes? Were they more homosexual than bisexual in character? Do these figures hold true for bisexuals in general? And how do these figures compare to the behavior patterns of homosexuals? It's known that there is a good deal of group activity among male homosexuals. Bisexual patterns may be closer to homosexual than heterosexual when it comes to group sex. It is also possible that the bisexual acts typically as a homosexual when in a homosexual situation that includes group sex, but heterosexually in heterosexual group sex situations. More research would be very helpful.

Two questions provided an insight into how bisexuals view themselves. Thirty-five percent had sought counseling for problems relating to their sexual orientation. On the other hand, over two-thirds said they would opt to be bisexual if they could begin life over. That many of the bisexuals had sought therapy for their difficulties isn't surprising, considering the negative connotation society places on this condition. But that so many *are* satisfied with it *is* surprising. Of those who would rather be bisexual if given a choice in a new life, only 28 percent had sought counseling for orientation problems. Of those who said they'd prefer to be heterosexual or homosexual, or did not respond, half had sought help for their sex-orientation difficulties.

Five of the questions on the questionnaire were designed for personal comment in the respondents' own words. To the first of these ("What are the main pleasures or advantages of being bisexual?"), answers did not vary significantly between male and female any more than they did on the same question answered orally at the Bisexual Forum. "More physical pleasure" and "more sexual variety" were the headliners, but somewhat different thoughts were also expressed, and are worth mentioning. One woman wrote, "Since recognizing and then accepting my bisexuality, I need no longer take the stance that I am repulsed by my own sex." A man expressed the same idea in more graphic terms: "I'm no longer afraid to touch men. I dig men and women. I think there are different sexual feelings one can have about each sex. I can enjoy without being disgusted by a cock and balls, which obviously a woman does not have."

Another important idea that emerges is the value of a broader range in self-definition. A young woman writes, "It's a good feeling to me not having to attach a strict label to myself sexually." A man answers: "I'm not limited in choice. I don't like unnecessary limits and labels placed on me."

The feeling of completeness is expressed with enough frequency to suggest the basis for a common bisexual awareness. "I feel complete in relationships with other human beings." And: "I find myself exploring closeness with people in a more intimate way."

An appreciation of "uniqueness" is expressed from many different points of view. "It's a learning process to enjoy the uniqueness of both sexes." And: "You get to experience a lot of people from many different backgrounds. Different types. Everyone is unique and that brings out different things in me."

In the above responses variety of experience was seen as an advantage. The next question, "What are the main problems or disadvantages of being bisexual?" explores the disadvantages in that variety. Social disapproval was the headliner here. "The most difficult thing is explaining to other people what I am. They just don't understand. It's funny, they understand variety in relation to other things in life–like, say, if you go to a big city public library you have more books to choose from than a small town library. But when it comes to sex, the most intelligent exclusively straight or gay person will just turn off on you. I really have kind of given up trying."

For most respondents, the main disadvantage was general social disapproval. However, for some individuals wider choice itself is an acute frustration. This is why some people flee cities for small towns or prefer to choose clothes without a wide range to select from. Variety can bring on indecision, and bisexuality surely affords increased social/sexual variety. "It's difficult to choose a lifestyle," one man said, echoing the feelings of a number of respondents. "I can't be open to everyone, and sometimes I'm not able to decide what I want or conform to what is expected of me."

For younger bisexuals the possibility of hurting parents or family is a pressure. "There is just no way my mother and father would understand. I have thought of moving across the country away from my family so they would never have to know."

The possibility of bisexuality interfering with monogamy and the possibility of being hurt by members of both sexes were two negative aspects of bisexuality for some. "I'm by nature a jealous person, and if the person I'm involved with is having other people, male or female, it can drive me right up the wall; and yet as a bisexual I understand, but understanding doesn't make the pain go away." And: "I have sex with other people of both sexes and I feel guilty because it makes my lover jealous. What's happened is that in order to survive I've become a really creative liar."

Having to lie, to conceal and not be completely what one is– even with close friends–is a black cloud hanging over the heads of many bisexuals. "I'm constantly aware no matter where I am or who I'm with that I must be careful with my secret. Yet I long sometimes just to blow it. Just to let it out and hang the cost. But I never do and the tension builds. I want to be respected at work and with friends, but my bisexual secret increases my fear of being rejected."

Promoting collective pride has become a way of validating group existence, for the sake of both its own self-definition and of how the group is viewed and defined by others. When I asked the question, "Do you take pride in being bisexual?" the answers were somewhat unexpected. "It's not a question of pride," one man wrote, "it's a question of being." This is a pretty ambiguous statement, yet when broken down I suspect it simply says that existence itself is enough and that *pride* in a state of being somehow diminishes that state. It is as though pride entailed an element of defensiveness. "No special pride. I simply am." And: "It's not a question of pride. It just is." One man summed up his sexuality in three words: "Yes. For myself." "Pride may be the wrong word," a woman wrote. "*Lucky* is more like it. I'm happy that I am open enough to be able to experience emotional or sexual love with both men and women."

These are all pointedly individual answers–not the responses of people who look to others before they speak. In this sense the bisexual is like an only child, to him or herself someone special, not a face in the crowd but *the* face in the crowd . . . "Yes; I feel special," a man wrote, "like being able to experience something others can't."

The bisexual has not been politicized. His or her condition is not yet a cause. In response to the pride question, one woman wrote two terse words: "Not applicable." Certainly not much group-think here.

Some people did give positive and negative responses to the same question. A few were uncertain. "Can't say. The issue is still unsettled in my mind. At times I'm up about it and at times I'm down and feel ashamed." But when the respondents were asked the direct question, "Do you have feelings of shame or guilt in being bisexual?" the majority answered no, though not all the no's were unqualified. "No. I have only some shame at the idea of being exposed." And "No. But I did before I really got into it." Those who answered yes were fewer in number but no less candid. "Yes. I feel shame, anxiety and guilt about homosexual pleasure, so I guess that applies to my bisexuality."

Though few felt shame and guilt directly, ambivalent feelings and confusion were often expressed in the responses given to the next and last question: "What are your feelings on your own bisexuality and bisexuality in general?" "I accept my own bisexuality but I'm not sure about other people's." And: "Ambivalent. Part of it is good and fulfilling, some of it is dehumanizing and demoralizing." One man expressed his confusion this way: "I'm still thinking deeply about my feeling." This way of looking at the question and not answering it directly was not unusual: "I don't feel that I have been involved long enough to offer opinions." And: "Part of me feels it's the only way to be and part of me feels that maybe it's no way to be. I don't know."

Though ambivalence and confusion characterized the responses of some, many expressed definite positive feelings: "It's a part of me–a happy aspect of me." "It's great." And "It's fine if that's what you choose to be." Some answers went into more detail. One woman wrote:

> I'm glad I met a guy who encouraged me to be me. Otherwise I might never have had the experience with women that I've had. I was afraid. I never felt that I was "abnormal" sexually, but I was afraid that other people would think so if they knew. Now I know different. I dig making love with women. I dig making love with men. It's nice to groove.

Another woman responded this way:

> Philosophically, I see bisexuality as the best of all possible
> worlds in terms of freedom and humanism. Personally I am
> bisexual and I feel I have always been and could not be any
> other way. I will have my preferences but will never deny
> myself the pleasure of feeling arousal toward men and women.
> I feel badly for people who have shut this fact out of their lives,
> much less those who have not even the slightest notion of its
> existence.

So the majority of people at the Forum had positive feelings
about their own bisexuality but felt the pressures of the heterosexual
and homosexual communities, which tended to create confusion,
doubt, and fear about themselves and their sexual inclinations.

If and when a large bisexual community emerges, it will probably change the bisexual's image of him/herself and change society's image too. As one young man wrote, tersely but eloquently,
"Should be no big deal, but is."

NOTES

Note 1

Some of the major findings on bisexuality are presented here,
starting with Kinsey et al., whose monumental survey is in some
respects still the most exhaustive ever undertaken. Kinsey found that
50 percent of the male population had never had an overt homosexual experience, nor reacted erotically on a psychological level toward
another man. So 50 percent of white American males were at 0 on
the Kinsey scale. Four percent were found to be completely homosexual. That leaves 46 percent in bisexual categories 1-5. Of course
one must keep in mind that this 46 percent includes all men beyond
puberty and might reflect only one sexual experience with the same
gender or minimal psychological or erotic feeling toward it.

Looking at men who had erotic reactions or actual experiences
over a three-year period in their lives between the ages of 16 and 55,
Kinsey found that:

- 70% of his sample were 0 (completely heterosexual) on the 0-6 heterosexual-homosexual scale
- 5% were 1 (incidentally homosexual)
- 7% were 2 (more than incidentally homosexual)
- 5% were 3 (equally heterosexual and homosexual)
- 3% were 4 (more than incidentally heterosexual)
- 2% were 5 (incidentally heterosexual)
- 8% were 6 (completely homosexual)

Combining categories 1-5, we see that 22 percent of the population can be considered bisexual if the above three-year experience is used as a basis for determination. (This three-year standard is arbitrary, and in my opinion not in any way really significant.) If we eliminate incidental experiences, this leaves 15 percent of the male population (categories 2, 3, and 4) as bisexual.

The ability to eroticize both genders is one dimension of bisexuality. Forty-six percent of the male population possesses this capability. If we consider only the ability to carry this capability into actual practice, the percentage of bisexuals in the population is 33 percent (Kinsey having found that 13 percent of the men had erotic reactions to other men without having had any actual experience).

For women, Kinsey found the incidence of homosexuality and bisexuality to be much lower than for men. For the 20 to 35 age group the following figures were established:

Category	Single	Married	Previously Married
0	61-75%	87-91%	75-81%
6	1-3%	–	1-3%
1-5	10-17%	8-10%	13-16%
2-4	4-8%	3%	5-7%
X	14-19%	1-3%	5-8%

Categories 0 to 6 have been defined before. Category X applies to women who did not respond erotically to either heterosexual or homosexual stimuli, and did not have overt physical contacts with individuals of either sex.

To quote Kinsey:

Among the females, the accumulative incidences of homosexual responses had ultimately reached 28 per cent; they had reached 50 per cent in the males. The accumulative incidences of overt contacts to the point of orgasm among the females had reached 13 per cent; among the males they had reached 37 per cent. This means that homosexual responses had occurred in about half as many females as males, and contacts which had proceeded to orgasm had occurred in about a third as many females as males.

Kinsey published his figures for men in 1948 and his figures for women in 1953. How do his statistics hold up after a quarter of a century? In the main they have not changed to any great degree.

Morton Hunt surveyed sexual behavior in the 1970s and published his findings in 1974 in *Sexual Behavior in the Seventies*. He found no increase in homosexual behavior on the part of his respondents. In fact, he felt that Kinsey's figures for males were somewhat too high, while his were too low. In general, they weren't far apart.

Two magazine surveys are of interest. (Though both had a very large response, care needs to be taken in their interpretation— voluntary responses to a magazine survey aren't representative of the total population.) In 1975, 100,000 women answered a *Redbook* survey on sexual pleasure. The responses were similar to Kinsey's: 10 percent of the separated or divorced women had sexual experience with other women; 4 percent of all who responded did so, with college-educated women having more overt lesbian activity than high school graduates.

In January 1977 *Psychology Today* published a survey on masculinity in which 68 percent of the male respondents considered themselves heterosexual and 6 percent homosexual, while 29 percent had some bisexual experience, of which 6 percent defined themselves as bisexual. These percentages are remarkably close to Kinsey's original statistics.

As mentioned above, in his major 1991 study of self-defined bisexuals, Ron Fox discussed when they first used the word "bisexual" to define themselves and to whom they disclosed this information.

Note 2

Using some of the statistics from Kinsey, there are 11 times as many bisexuals as homosexuals if capability of erotic feelings toward both sexes is the criterion used. If one defines a bisexual in Kinsey's survey of men between the ages of 16 and 55 as someone who had sexual experiences with both sexes during the three-year period preceding being interviewed, then there are twice as many bisexual males as homosexual males (defining homosexual as fitting into categories 5 and 6 on Kinsey's scale).

The 1993 study by John Billy et al. as well as some of the international surveys in the early 1990s indicated that the bisexual population is between 2 and 3 times as large as the homosexual population.

Note 3

There have been a number of studies on homosexuals both in their subculture and in the population in general. Some of these have asked respondents questions about heterosexual activity–in other words, bisexuality. The studies quite consistently found that 50 percent of male homosexuals, whether they are self-defined as such or part of the homosexual subculture (bars, dances, or gay organizations), have in their histories experienced heterosexual activity. This figure was constant in the 1973 Saghir and Robins survey, a survey by Rick Shur of male homosexuals at New York City gay dances in 1974, and even a large 1974 German survey by Dannecker and Reiche. For female homosexuals the figure is higher, with over 75 percent of the "lesbian" respondents having had heterosexual experiences.

Dividing people for purposes of study into only two groups, "heterosexual" and "homosexual," which is done most of the time, and defining all people at gay dances or all men found in gay bars as "homosexual," has the effect of lumping bisexuals into these groups and makes interpretation of the results extremely difficult. For example, 96 percent of the respondents in the Dannecker and Reiche survey were considered to be homosexuals in that at the time of the survey 83 percent had no heterosexual activity at all, while another 13 percent had only incidental heterosexual activity.

The authors eliminate the bisexual category altogether, explaining it as a way station to homosexuality or as a social subterfuge. But how then should we interpret the fact that 56 percent of the men had previous sexual experience with women while another 10 percent were or had previously been married? Or consider this: in Shur's survey of men at gay dances the respondents were asked if they had a strong preference for their own sex. This question was asked "in order to establish that the respondents were gay." Ninety-six percent answered yes to this question. But then what do the following responses mean: 30 percent were attracted to women enough to consider having sexual relations with them, and 60 percent had defined themselves as bisexual at one time or another.

There seems to be no doubt that a large percentage of those considered homosexual in sociological studies would more properly be considered bisexuals–including many of those who have defined themselves as homosexuals. This would seem to be a fact of long standing. In a study of gay couples who had been living together at least one year, Drs. McWhirter and Mattison found that only 15 percent could be considered to be in the 6 category on the Kinsey scale; 25 percent had previously lived with a woman from six months to a year, and 65 percent had had at least one heterosexual experience after puberty, most having had many. Though at the time of the study few respondents had any concurrent heterosexual activity, 75 percent had occasional heterosexual fantasies and only 25 percent exclusively homosexual fantasies.

Note 4

Kinsey found that 2 percent of the older men and close to 10 percent of the younger ones (ages 16-25) had homosexual experience while married in the previous five years. He stated that for a number of reasons the figures for older men were probably in reality higher. Hunt found a 1 percent bisexual experience rate in the previous year, the same percentage as in the 1991 Dutch study of van Zessen and Sandford. The three figures correspond in the sense that a lower figure has to be expected for one year's activity compared to activity spread over five years. There are no statistics on cumulative numbers. For women the number is lower. Kinsey found that 8 to 10 percent of married women between the ages of 20 and 35 had bisexual experience each year. For active incidence the figure would be around 1 percent (Hunt). The figures for separated and divorced men and women are of course higher. When one looks at the statistics for homosexual groups, the following marriage figures apply: anywhere from 1 to 5 percent of self-identified homosexuals are presently married. As for previously married homosexuals, the figures are 5 to 24 percent. Self-defined female homosexuals were more often previously married than male ones. In her survey of self-identified bisexual women, Janet Bode found that 17 percent were married at the time of the survey.

Chapter 9

The Bisexual in History and the Arts

THE BISEXUAL IN HISTORY

All too frequently, people fail or refuse to recount, or even re-member, the past–the good and the bad–the way it really was. Instead, we revise and misrepresent it to serve current needs, wishes, fantasies, or political purposes, or to shore up cherished values. History becomes a tool, a weapon to control the present and mold the future. For a long time, for example, the Battle of Little Big Horn was served up to white American as a story of American soldiers who "died with their boots on," bathed in glory, instead of in stupidity, cruelty, and pointless bloodshed. By such historical sleight of hand, the descendants of Sitting Bull, right down to the present generation of displaced Indians, are more easily dismissed and forgotten.

Men's age-old denial of women's achievements is another glaring example of history used as a weapon. Even though most historians agree that Elizabeth I was the finest monarch England ever had, women's fitness to rule a nation is still often challenged–and not only by men but even by women who have come to believe in the lie.

In the country that produced the Magna Carta and the parliamentary system of government, Oscar Wilde was put on trial in the 1890s for homosexuality, which exposed a homosexual London underground that included stable boys, clerks, domestic servants and the like. Wilde was convicted and sent to prison. He was branded a homosexual in his time. But he is also exploited as a homosexual in our time. Oscar Wilde was not a homosexual. He was a bisexual. In *Oscar Wilde*, H. Montgomery Hyde writes:

. . . we know that at the outset of their married life Wilde was deeply in love with his wife and that they experienced normal sexual intercourse, which resulted in the birth of their two sons. Indeed, he seems to have been an enthusiastic lover. To Sherard, whom he chanced to meet during the honeymoon in Paris, he spontaneously expatiated upon the physical joys of wedlock. And on the occasion of his first separation from his wife, some months later, when he was lecturing in Edinburgh, he wrote to her:

"Here I am; and you at the Antipodes: O execrable fates that keep our lips from kissing, though our souls are one. . . . The messages of the gods to each other travel not by pen and ink, and indeed your bodily presence here would not make you more real: for I feel your fingers in my hair and your cheek brushing mine. The air is full of the music of your voice, my soul and body seem no longer mine, but mingled in some exquisite ecstasy with yours. I feel incomplete without you."*

Before he married, Wilde had developed a reputation at Oxford as a man not only interested in women but highly enamored of them. His casual affairs were many and his love affairs were deeply felt. Montgomery Hyde continues:

His first serious love affair during this early period . . . was with Florence Balcombe, a girl four years younger than himself. Oscar's passion for Florrie lasted two years–"the sweetest of all the years of my youth," so he told her afterwards–and no doubt he wished to marry her.

Before his interest in male sexual partners developed, Wilde had already achieved a reputation as a writer and lecturer not only in England but also in the United States. Had he died during this time we would remember him as a "normal" if somewhat flamboyant heterosexual male. To some, he might have been considered a bisexual because an interest in male physical beauty can be seen in some of his early poems. "He may well have been unaware of its

---

*See note on permission page.

significance at the same time," Hyde writes, "as his inclinations gradually became bisexual."

The highly regarded contemporary writer, Gore Vidal, has for years been the target of homosexual gossip. One gets the impression that this bothers him only to the degree that it is not true. He has publicly defended his bisexuality. In 1974, in the afterward to *The City and the Pillar*, he wrote:

> . . . All human beings are bisexual. Conditioning, opportunity and habit account finally (and mysteriously) for sexual preference, and homosexualists are quite as difficult to generalize about as heterosexualists. They range from the transvestite who believes himself to be Bette Davis to the perfectly ordinary citizen who regards boys with the same uncomplicated lust that his brother regards girls.
>
> When legal and social pressures against homosexuality are particularly severe, homosexualists can become neurotic, in much the same way that Jews and Negroes do in a hostile environment. Yet a man who enjoys sensual relations with his own sex is not, by definition, neurotic. In any event, categorizing is impossible. Particularly when one considers that most homosexualists marry and become fathers, which makes them, technically, bisexuals, a condition whose existence is firmly denied by at least one school of psychiatry on the odd ground that a man must be one thing or the other, which is demonstrably untrue. Admittedly, no two things are equal, and so a man is bound to prefer one specific to another, but that does not mean that under the right stimulus, and at another time, he might not accommodate himself to both.
>
> . . . In any case, sex of any sort is neither right nor wrong. It is.

We've had Kinsey's heterosexual-homosexual scale for over 40 years now, the Klein Sexual Orientation Grid for over ten. We should use them more often. They could help us clear up the matter of who is and who is not heterosexual, homosexual, or bisexual. Every human being has a right to be judged intelligently for what he or she *really* is–in all its breadth and complexity–and not be chopped down by society's clumsy ax to fit its procrustean bed. What follows is a list of notable people, both past and present, whose sexual identities have either been distorted or obscured by our stubborn insistence on the theory of either-or.

Historically, these people tend to be labeled homosexual; in some few cases, heterosexual. In truth they were, and are, most assuredly bisexual. This ongoing propagation of the either-or standard at the expense of the truth is another example of the manipulation of history–an enforcement, in a sense, of the people's right *not* to know. When Galileo in the seventeenth century was offered torture and death as the alternative to renouncing his endorsement of the Copernican cosmology, he chose to live–and the people's "right" not to know that the earth revolves around the sun was carried forward. The theory of the nonexistence of bisexuality is likewise an historical distortion of the truth.

Bisexuals–Past and Present

Alexander the Great	Janis Joplin
Pietro Aretino	John Maynard Keynes
Baba Ram Dass (Richard Alpert)	Louis XIII
Joan Baez	Robin Maugham
Tallulah Bankhead	W. Somerset Maugham
David Bowie	Kate Millett
Francis Bacon	Harold Nicolson
Julius Caesar	Charles Reich
Catullus	Vita Sackville-West
Colette	Maria Schneider
Philip, Duke of Orleans	Ted Shawn
Edward II	Bessie Smith
André Gide	Socrates
Henry III	Dorothy Thompson
Horace	Paul Verlaine
Janis Ian	Gore Vidal
James I	Oscar Wilde
Elton John	Virginia Woolf

The history of bisexuality has gone mostly unrecorded. Its records are sparse. To find material I had to search through *homosexual* history. From there I teased out those people who were actually bisexual rather than homosexual. Historical knowledge of bisexuality will not emerge from the shadows until people at least admit to its reality.

If the reader senses a somewhat strident tone here, the writer pleads guilty; in mitigation, I will say that the stridency is only the companion of the excitement I feel that the bisexual idea's time has perhaps come at last, that our culture is ready at last to recognize bisexuality's existence.

A way to begin demonstrating the reality of bisexuality is to encourage a focus on the homosexual or heterosexual *act* as opposed to the homosexual or heterosexual *person*. If, for instance, an English businessman travels to France to do business and while there uses what he knows of the French language, we do not therefore call him a Frenchman. The act of speaking French may make him bilingual, but he remains an Englishman. Crossing the language barrier is an act that in no way defines the person except to say that he speaks more than one language. An example more to the point is that of the playwright Tennessee Williams, who was "homosexual" all of his life. In his autobiography, *Memoirs*, he described having had at least one sexual encounter with a woman. His action (quite successful by his account) was most decidedly heterosexual, but from his autobiography he appears to be almost every level homosexual despite it. Yet there is also some room for him on the bisexual list, because he has a capacity for heterosexual action.

Mr. Williams' single act will not get him to be called a heterosexual–whereas *any* homosexual activity on the part of any heterosexual is often enough for him or her to be thought of as homosexual. So the "either-or" view really works in one direction only–to transport everyone who is not 100 percent heterosexual to the homosexual camp. Which, of course, as seen in the case of Oscar Wilde, further obfuscates the identifying of overall behavior as bisexual . . . which is how every other individual on my list is also correctly describable.

These bisexuals were chosen for the list because, being famous, there is documented proof of the sexual preference. Still, this would not be true for, say, Michelangelo, even though he is certainly famous. On circumstantial evidence alone, Michelangelo was a bisexual, but we remain less than certain of it because there is no hard evidence to prove what he was sexually. A razor's-edge line separates hard evidence and conjecture. One century's supposition can be another century's firm conclusion. A hundred years from now, Michelangelo might be put on the list; new evidence may be unearthed.

History keeps historical figures alive in the sense that our views of them are subject to change. We do not let them rest in peace. In some cases, 1000 or 2000 years is not enough to settle all the questions, to lay the case to rest. This is particularly true of Alexander the Great, the first name on the list.

Today, Alexander is thought of as more homosexual than heterosexual. Yet despite what Mary Renault terms his "normal Greek bisexuality," only twenty years ago Richard Burton, because of the homosexual taboos extant at the time, played him as a heterosexual in an otherwise remarkably accurate Hollywood film. Alexander has been claimed by both heterosexuals and homosexuals. In Alexander's case, the people's "right not to know" has been formidable. It is interesting to note that since the emergence of "Gay Lib," the homosexual's right not to know, such as in the case of Alexander, is every bit as strong as the heterosexual's. But Alexander, though Macedonian, was a Greek culturally, intellectually, emotionally, and sexually. He lived according to the normal Greek bisexuality of his time.

He lived 33 years, not long. If there is any truth at all in the theory that the individual shapes history (as opposed to the Tolstoyan view that events create the individual), then Alexander, who at the age of 16 was appointed Regent of Macedon by his father, Philip II, is a towering example. In his teens he served under his father in war and was appointed to the rank of general. By the time he reached his early twenties his legend was established. Two thousand years after his death, Afghan chiefs would claim to be his direct descendants.

His motivation for conquering the world was to make the world Greek. His enemies, who might hold out against his armies, would quake at the news that he himself was on the march. As a warrior he viewed the impossible as a personal challenge. In Sogdiana he and his army were faced with what appeared to be an impossible ascent up what was known as the Sogdian Rock–in Mary Renault's words, "high, sheer, and riddled at the top with caves well stocked with

food and water. . . . The single path to the top was entirely comman-
ded from above. The area was under snow." Had Alexander not
undertaken the task of conquering Sogdian Rock, he would not
have seen and met Roxane, the daughter of the chief, Oxyartes. He
fell in love with her at first sight, spared the people and the town,
and asked her father for her hand in marriage.

Roxane married a man with but five years to live. During that
time, Alexander was continually off on another siege; it is apparent
that he did not give her much of his time. After his marriage to
Roxane, he took a second wife, Barsine-Stateira, the daughter of
Darius. Judging by the accounts of the marriage ceremony, it was so
lavish that from that time on Barsine had to be regarded as his chief
wife. What Roxane said about this second marriage is unknown but
her feelings were expressed in blood when, during the year following Alexander's death, she put Barsine to death and had the body
thrown into a well. Thirteen years later she herself was murdered,
together with her son, Alexander IV.

The heterosexual side of Alexander's bisexuality is apparent
from the above facts. His homosexual side is just as clear. In defeat-
ing King Darius III of Persia, one of Alexander's spoils was Ba-
goas, the youngest of the king's court eunuchs, a boy of exceptional
beauty and an accomplished singer and dancer. Their close attach-
ment lasted until Alexander's death. But it was Hephaestion who
shared a lifelong love relationship, both emotional and sexual, with
Alexander. They met early in youth and Hephaestion is described as
being taller and even better looking than the handsome Alexander.
Beginning his career simply as a member of the King's own cavalry
regiment, Hephaestion was promoted eventually to the highest military and civil rank and was never defeated in any of his independent
assignments. His unexpected death nearly unseated Alexander's
reason. For 24 hours Alexander lay on the body until his friends
dragged him off by force; for three days he fasted, could only lie
weeping, and was unapproachable. He forbade all music in court
and camp, ordered mourning in every city of the empire, and dedi-
cated to Hephaestion his late regiment, to bear his name in perpetu-
ity.

Because of his culture, Alexander's open bisexuality was not at
all unusual. When we think of Alexander, we do not focus on his

sex life. It was part of the man, as it is part of all living creatures, but that is not why he is remembered, nor why he was Alexander the Great. This is not true of another household name on our list.

Oscar Wilde was a child of far from ordinary parents, particularly the father, who also figured in a sensational trial. Sir William Wilde, famous as a doctor and an intellect, and the possessor of an abnormally strong sex drive, was accused of having violated a woman patient.

Oscar, Sir William's second son, grew to be even more celebrated, and perhaps possessed an equally demanding sex drive. Despite Oscar Wilde's enduring importance as a playwright, poet, novelist, and wit, we continue to think of this flamboyant, even outrageous man in connection with his sexual drive. This was directed at both genders, but Wilde was a sequential bisexual. For the first 32 or so years of his life he lived as a lusty, enthusiastic heterosexual, and for the next 14 years, until his death in Paris in 1900, he lived as an equally lusty and enthusiastic homosexual.

Wilde was charged with and tried for homosexual practices, found guilty, and sentenced to two years imprisonment with hard labor. By the time he was released he was broken, both as an artist and as a man. Wilde was found guilty of committing specific acts abhorrent by the moral standards of the time. Our culture, in its collective and selective memory, translates those acts into an image of an exclusively homosexual man, despite Wilde's active sexual pursuit of women well into his early thirties. Wilde enjoyed women on both emotional and sexual levels; he fell in love and married, not out of convenience to cover his homosexuality but because he was deeply in love with his wife, as was Alexander with Roxane. That both of these loves cooled doesn't diminish their validity in the lifetimes of the two men any more than, say, Picasso's change of women every ten years or so in the course of a very long heterosexual life means that he loved *only* the last woman living with him when he died.

While in prison, in hopes of gaining an early release on his sentence, Wilde wrote a petition to the Home Secretary. Although it puts forward what we would call today a plea of temporary insanity, it actually does a great deal more. Entitled *De Profundis,* it strongly reinforces Wilde's reputation as a literary giant and shows him to have been a devoted family man who loved his children and felt deeply the agonies brought on them and his wife by his conduct. That he was using his family in an effort to secure his release is obvious. But that he *had* them to use, while behind bars for committing homosexual acts, would seem of paramount significance, and reason enough in itself to view him as a bisexual.

Future historians who report the sexual history of our time (loosely dating from the publication of Kinsey's first study in 1948) will have a better-paved road to travel than past ones did. Past generations were for the most part reticent about revealing sexual preference if it differed from the norm. Indeed, in general the only way students of history can be sure that their subjects had sex at all is if they produced children. We can, for instance, speculate about Michelangelo's bisexuality, or ponder Lytton Strachey's view of Queen Victoria's husband, Albert, as a bisexual, but the open admission of bisexuality by any person, prominent or otherwise, from the past is exceedingly rare.

"I've been such a fool," W. Somerset Maugham said to his nephew Robin Maugham (quoted by the latter in his book *Escape from the Shadows*), "and the awful thing is that if I had my life to live all over again I'd probably make exactly the same mistakes."

"What mistakes?" his nephew asked.

"M-my greatest one was this," the author stammered. "I tried to persuade myself that I was three-quarters normal and that only one-quarter of me was queer–whereas really it was the other way around."

W. Somerset Maugham was an enormously prolific and successful writer–a man who put his creative shoulder to the wheel with such strength and assiduity that year after year he produced novels, plays, short stories, and essays that for the most part read as well today as when written. *Of Human Bondage*, his first successful novel, is still widely read and enjoyed some 50 years after its first publication. *Cakes and Ale*, his own favorite novel, is so skillful in its narrative execution and so deeply felt that it is praised by critics who are less than enthusiastic about the body of Maugham's work as a whole. There is little question that those two books mentioned above, *The Razor's Edge*, and nearly all the short stories will live for many years.

Maugham's bisexuality did not manifest itself until around the year 1908, when he was 34 years old. Eleven years earlier, with the success of his first novel he had abandoned thoughts of a medical career in order to write. His plays quickly earned him acclaim and a great deal of money. By the time he fell in love with an actress (identified only by the first name of Nan) he was financially independent. "She had the most beautiful smile I had ever seen on a human being," Maugham said of this woman. He was in love with her for eight years. While she was appearing in a play in Chicago, he asked for her hand in marriage, but she had promised it to the son of an earl, whom she married a few weeks later. The loss haunted Maugham all of his life. The character of Rosie in *Cakes and Ale* is based on Nan.

W. Menard quotes Maugham in *The Two Worlds of Somerset Maugham:*

> No, I was never what is known as a "ladies man." I didn't have the looks or the disposition, or, I might add, the time to play at it. In my company I found most women uncomfortable and somewhat contentious, somehow sensing that I found them transparent and was quite aware of all their grubby little tricks. I think that most women went to bed with me out of curiosity, or accepted me as a temporary lover to maintain their standard of copulating only with well-known and well-to-do gentlemen, or for personal gain.

Because Maugham viewed himself as less than attractive to women, he was circumspect about approaching them. That he conducted a number of affairs with women despite this is evidenced by his statement that no one need worry about his autobiography revealing the names of "the number of women still living, with whom I have had affairs."

He married once. It was not a happy alliance. Her name was Gwendolen Syrie Barnardo. Maugham had been unattached, affluent, and vulnerable. After acquiring him as a lover, Miss Barnardo accused him of making her pregnant. She attempted suicide, forcing the issue of marriage. Although Maugham was not sure the child was his, he said, "I could not bear to think what its future would be if I didn't marry its mother." The marriage lasted ten years before ending in divorce.

Robin Maugham, also a bisexual, picks up the story: "But quite apart from the obvious incompatibility of temperaments, the marriage was bound to have failed–because even before he married Syrie, Willie [Maugham's nickname] had met Gerald."

Gerald served as Maugham's secretary and housekeeper–services, in the Victorian society, that a good wife ordinarily would perform. Gerald ran the house, he kept the accounts, and helped set the tone of general hospitality at social gatherings. ". . . but also–" Robin Maugham writes, "it was obvious to me–he depended on Gerald to produce young boys who could creep into the Mauresque by the back door and sleep with him."

If Maugham was three-quarters "queer" and one-quarter "normal," there must have been a lot of boys. During his lifetime, the general public's image of Maugham was that of the English gentleman, the club member, the successful writer, a bit stiff but not without charm. If he was not committed to a kind of a sexual bachelorhood, he was certainly committed to a bumbling kind of heterosexuality. Now, in his grave, Maugham is being wrongly labeled a restless, distraught, even miserable, homosexual.

"No man is of one piece," he said to his nephew. "He's made up of selfishness and generosity, cruelty and kindness." Diversity in his artistic vision was reflected in his bisexual life. Somerset Maugham was a rare exception: in his time few actually stated their bisexual inclination. *Familiar Faces, Hidden Lives*, the title of the autobiography of Dr. Howard Brown, a homosexual, expresses it aptly. For bisexuals, the "closet door" is usually even more firmly shut.

Such is the case with Sidonie Gabrielle Colette, known to the world simply as Colette. She lived to the age of 81, having written over 70 books from 1900 to the time of her death in 1954. She was honored not only with the Grand Cross of the Legion of Honor and election to the presidency of the Goncourt Academy but also with a state funeral, the only woman in French history to be so honored. Her novel *Chèri* is her best known, although in the United States it is perhaps topped by *Gigi*, which was also adapted as a play and as a musical for both stage and screen.

Colette married three times in her life. Her first marriage at the age of 20 to Henri Gauthier-Villars lasted 13 years. Six years later she fell in love with the editor Henri de Jouvenel, and in the year following her marriage to him she gave birth to her only child, a daughter also named Colette. Her second marriage was dissolved 12 years later. Then once again she fell in love and married, this time to Maurice Goudeket, a writer, who to the end she always called her best friend.

Accounts of these heterosexual affairs of the heart are available in any Colette biography. But the homosexual aspects of her bisexuality are always stated with qualifications, not because they did not exist, I believe, but because of the usual stigma attached to bisexuality, resulting in its consignment to nonexistence.

When Colette left her first husband she was befriended by the Marquise de Belboeuf, known as "Missy." Missy, who dressed as a man and loved women exclusively, took Colette to her house, where she stayed for a number of months. In her 1975 biography of Colette, Yvonne Mitchell writes: "Though Colette shared a bed with her friend, her relationship with Missy remained ambiguous." In *Willy, Colette et Moi*, Bonmarriage claimed that Colette had an affair with an actress named Polaire, with Missy, and with a number of other women. In her first biography of Colette, Margaret Crosland attempted to deny these facts: "Colette was talked of as a Lesbian because she was curious about women and found them just as interesting as men, in certain cases, more interesting." However, in her second biography, published in 1973, Crosland describes a deep emotional and physical friendship between Missy and Colette: "The relationship between the two women is perhaps best described as 'amitie amoureuse,' a term much more expressive than 'lesbianism,' of which there is no simple definition."

Colette's works deal mainly with the relationships between men and women. Throughout her novels and essays, however, she also deals with bisexual attachments and loves. Consistently, she wrote only about what she knew. It is clear that she knew very well the breadth and depth of human love.

One of the high points in the history of Western civilization was attained in ancient Greece. In that culture, bisexuality existed openly and was looked upon with favor. Sensuality was held in high esteem, together with its concomitant aspects of beauty and love. Sensual enjoyment was recognized by the great thinkers of Greece as a legitimate ideal, necessary for happiness. Although social laws were rigorous, sensuality and its manifestations were not condemned by public opinion. Higher ethics, combined with love of the senses, created a superior culture.

Greek men assigned women two roles—mother and courtesan. In the great majority were the mothers; marriage and motherhood were highly honored. The wife had complete management and control of domestic affairs and the bringing up of the children—the girls until marriage, and the boys until early puberty, when control was taken over by men. The woman's role was subordinate to the man's. Education, especially in the Hellenic culture, was generally available only to the male. Girls were taught spinning and weaving by their mothers. The Greeks believed that the woman's place was in her own quarters, where she had no need of book learning.

In *Civilization* Clive Bell provides an excellent description of the two roles:

> . . . the housewife is a worker; and the Athenian housewife was recognized as such. She was treated with the respect due to every honest and capable worker; but she did not, because by the nature of her interests and occupations she could not, belong to the highly civilized and civilizing elite. . . . [The Athenians] divided women into two groups: a large active group consisting of those excellent, normal creatures whose predominant passion is for child-rearing and house-management; and a small idle group composed of women with a taste for civilization. To the latter went, or tended to go, girls of exceptional intelligence and sensibility, born with a liking for independence and the things of the mind.

To the latter group, the courtesans or Hetairai, the Athenians offered respect, adoration, and intimacy. They were distinguished by their wit and intellect. As Clive Bell further describes them, "They were as much admired in public as adored in private. They flirted with Socrates and his friends and sat at the feet of Plato and Epicurus."

The story is told of a young man who did not get up from his place before Dercyllidas, the famous but unmarried Spartan general, saying: "You have begotten no one who will later make way for me." His attitude was typical; in Greek civilization marriage was regarded as a duty to the gods so that the citizen left behind descendants to ensure the continued existence of the state. In fact, a law promulgated by Lycurgus punished unmarried men.

Not only was the love of man for woman exalted in this culture but also the love of man for man, which was widespread and idealized. In *Sexual Life in Ancient Greece*, Hans Licht writes:

> To facilitate the understanding of the Hellenic love of boys, it will be as well to say something about the Greek ideal of beauty. . . . Antiquity treated the man, and the man only, as the focus of all intellectual life. This explains why the bringing up and development of girls was neglected in a way we can hardly understand; but the boys, on the other hand, were supposed to continue their education much later than is usual with us. The most peculiar custom, according to our ideas, was that every man attracted to him some boy or youth and, in the intimacy of daily life, acted as his counsellor, guardian, and friend, and prompted him in all manly virtues . . . it is by no means surprising if the sensual love of the Greeks was also directed towards their boys and that they sought and found in intercourse with them community of soul. There was added to the ideal of beauty the richer and more highly developed intellectual talents of the boys, which made rational conversation possible. . . .

Plato has this to say in the *Symposium:*

> . . . For I cannot say what greater benefit can fall to the lot of a young man than a virtuous lover and to the lover than a beloved youth. . . . If then there were any means whereby a state or army could be formed of lovers and favorites, they would administer affairs better than all others, provided they abstain from all disgraceful deed and compete with one another in honest rivalry.

The love of the Greeks for youth was elevated and sacred. So was Sappho's inclination for her own sex. A favorite philosophical subject in the ancient literature is the question of whether the love of a man for a woman should always be preferred to the love of a man for a boy. In *Erotes*, Lycinus answers the question in the following words:

> Marriage is for men a life-pressing necessity and a precious thing, if it is a happy one; but the love of boys, so far as it courts the sacred rights of affection, is in my opinion a result of practical wisdom. Therefore let marriage be for all, but let the love of boys remain alone the privilege of the wise.

Many historians feel that bisexuality was an important factor in Greece's grandeur. At least in antiquity we note a civilized culture that did not feel threatened by the bisexuality of its citizens.

The thread of bisexual history does not end with the fall of Athens, but as a civilizing influence it becomes nearly invisible after the death of Alexander. Though always practiced, bisexuality was never again accorded a recognized role in the nurture of Western civilization. But some 2200 years later, one small corner of Western civilization proved exceptional.

One day in 1904 the young Lytton Strachey, who would achieve fame and critical acclaim as the biographer of Queen Elizabeth and Queen Victoria, came to tea at 46 Garden Square in Bloomsbury, invited by Vanessa and Virginia Stephen, the daughters of Sir Leslie Stephen, who had died in February of that year. Thus began what came to be called the Bloomsbury Group. Vanessa would marry Clive Bell and Virginia would move to a house nearby, 29 Fitzroy Square. She would later marry Leonard Woolf. "If ever such an entity as Bloomsbury existed," Clive Bell wrote, "these sisters with their houses in Garden and Fitzroy Squares were the heart of it."

It was in the ground-floor study of Virginia's home that these friends assembled on Thursday evenings for whiskey, buns, cocoa, and conversation. The mood of these congregations was fed by the awareness of those present that they were living at a time when all the benefits of breeding, education, intelligence, financial independence, and leisure could be mobilized to the fullest. They developed a standard of masculine and feminine values directed toward an ascendancy of enlightenment; no man or woman would be seen in the stereotypical roles thrust upon them by society. No member of the Bloomsbury Group was without some degree of bisexual experience. That they produced an enormous body of important work attests, in part, to the bisexual and androgynous ideals by which they lived.

No true godhead existed for the Bloomsbury Group. But G. E. Moore, the Cambridge philosopher and author of *Principia Ethica*, was held in a kind of reserved reverence. His philosophy also embodied the androgynous ideal so dear to the hearts of those who gathered together on Thursday nights. Reason and passion that excluded violence were seen as equally important ideals. The purpose of the Cambridge humanism behind Moore's philosophy was simply "the spread of civilization."

It is with wonder that we look today on the whole group, both for how much these bisexual writers, thinkers, painters and critics accomplished intellectually and artistically, and for the reconciliation they achieved between the masculine and feminine aspects of being.

Who were they, this group that held that the external world of action and material things, however, important, was but a single candle next to the sun of the spirit, the virtues of courage, tolerance, and honesty, the individual expression of emotion and intellect? They were friends before they were famous, before any of them had learned to do much more than nourish one another with brilliant conversation that supported and fed their individual talents. Virginia Woolf was to write in her book *The Death of the Moth*, "The only criticism worth having is that which is spoken over wine glasses and coffee cups late at night, flushed out on the spur of the moment by people passing who have not time to finish their sentences."

Together with Roger Fry, Clive Bell first introduced the postimpressionist painters to a scandalized London. John Maynard Keynes, another Bloomsbury Group member, became *the* economist of his age and, according to some, of ours as well. Lytton Strachey has been called the biographer's biographer and the most readable writer ever to have worked in that form. Leonard Woolf made the Hogarth Press into one of the most impressive publishing houses of all time, and he himself was a gifted and socially conscious writer. There was E. M. Forster, whose credits need hardly be enumerated. In the National Portrait Gallery in London hang, testimonies to the impressive talents of painters Duncan Grant and Vanessa Bell. At the center of the Group was the illuminating genius of Virginia Woolf. They were extraordinary, individually and collectively, and like the Greeks their bisexuality was a concomitant to their achievement. The "Bloomsberries" were almost all–if not all–bisexual not only in action but in psychological outlook. As with the Greeks, it is this outlook that is of special interest. The sexual polarization common to the "Bloomsberries' " time–and essentially to ours as well–was viewed by the Group as undesirable and even destructive, and remarkably, they managed to transcend it.

In *Toward a Recognition of Androgyny*, Carolyn G. Heilbrun writes of Lytton Strachey:

> He at least understood that sweetness without intelligence and forcefulness is as powerless as masculine domination without the balance of femininity is destructive. In those who accomplish much, the elements are frequently so mixed that mankind might stand up and say: there is a human being.

It is the vision of this extraordinary balance in every man and woman that distinguishes the Bloomsbury Group and gives it a strong place in the history of bisexuality. Ms. Heilbrun also writes of Virginia Woolf:

> Holtby's particular contribution as a critic of Woolf is to have perceived Woolf's central vision as embodying less an inner tension between masculine and feminine inclinations than a search for a new synthesis. . . . The sight of two people, a man and a woman, in a taxi, which seemed to Woolf a metaphor for the conjoining of the two sexes rather than the separation of them into antagonistic forces, was seized upon by Holtby to stand for Woolf's androgynous vision.

Thousands of years passed between the Greeks and the "Bloomsberries." Nearly a century separates Oscar Wilde from Gore Vidal. In digging into the bisexual past this very amateur historian has for the most part hit bedrock only a few feet down. That there is treasure beyond is certain. Whether it can be unearthed eventually will depend, I suspect, upon our present and future commitment to discovering the truth of human sexuality in general. Only half a century separates Sigmund Freud from the Kinsey report. The near future seems promising.

THE BISEXUAL AS PORTRAYED IN THE ARTS

There has been considerable ambivalence toward the figure of the bisexual in the arts, including literature and the cinema. Consider two highly successful films of serious intent, *Women in Love* and *Sunday Bloody Sunday*. Both have a visibly bisexual axis at the center of their narrative lines. *Sunday Bloody Sunday*, from an original screenplay by Penelope Gilliatt, deals with people and events. *Women in Love*, an adaptation of the D. H. Lawrence novel, deals more with ideas. *Women in Love* portrays bisexuality more convincingly than *Sunday Bloody Sunday* because of its focus on the bisexual idea as opposed to the bisexual in action, in "reality." All too often, the "realistic" treatment of a subject merely means the unwitting assumption of present-day prejudices and myopia–such as the myth of nonexistence. It is the artist who seeks the truth, rather than the artist who shows the reality, who has given bisexuality its most convincing credential.

The bisexual role in *Sunday Bloody Sunday* falls to the character of Bob, a shallow, vapidly attractive young man who controls simultaneously the love of two people, a respected London doctor who is also homosexual and a woman in her mid-thirties, divorced and nothing short of fascinating in her unrelenting search for direction and purpose in a stagnant existence. Both the doctor and the woman are full-blown, beautifully realized characters, sympathetic and invested with intelligence and charm. The weak link in the film is the character of Bob, the bisexual who is portrayed as so deficient of feeling one cannot help but wonder why the woman and the doctor are so enamored of him. Within the story he is pale, self-absorbed, and flimsy almost to the point of not being there, though without him there is no story at all. In short, he is a major character whose ambiguity reduces him to minor effect. He is, in short, and in the sense of *character*, nonexistent.

The combined talents of the people who made this film are impressive. It is an intelligent, compassionate film, put together by people normally associated with creative, responsible work. To every other character, they give proper definition. Why, then, do they come a cropper when dealing with the bisexual? Is it a conscious hatchet job? I don't think so. The film and its makers are too honest for that. But, as stated above, even gifted, well-intentioned artists are conditioned by the same all-pervasive myth of nonexistence as their audience.

Women in Love succeeds in conveying its bisexual idea through the character of Rupert Birkin (based on D. H. Lawrence himself), a young man who seeks the love of the girl Ursula on the one hand and his friend Gerald on the other.

Set in the early 1900s, the final scene of the novel and the film has Ursula and Birkin sitting in a country mill quietly talking:

"Did you need Gerald?" she asked . . .

"Yes," he said.

"Aren't I enough for you?" she asked.

"No," he said. "You are enough for me, as far as a woman is concerned. You are all women to me. But I wanted a man friend, as eternal as you and I are eternal."

"Why aren't I enough?" she said. "You are enough for me. I don't want anybody else but you. Why isn't it the same with you?"

"Having you, I can live all my life without anybody else, any other sheer intimacy. But to make it complete, really happy, I wanted eternal union with a man too: another kind of love," he said.

"I don't believe it," she said. "It's an obstinacy, a theory, a perversity."

"Well–" he said.

"You can't have two kinds of love. Why should you!"

"It seems as if I can't," he said. "Yet I wanted it."

"You can't have it, because it's false, impossible," she said.

"I don't believe that," he answered.

Birkin's is, so to speak, a bisexual voice in the wilderness. We feel for him as we do not for Bob in *Sunday Bloody Sunday*, even if our personal view of sexual intimacy is dictated by an "either-or" stance, because the bisexual idea here exists a meaningful distance away from the bisexual reality: in *Sunday Bloody Sunday* we see Bob in love scenes with both the doctor and the woman; *Women in Love* shows only heterosexual sex directly. The bisexual extension is represented in a wrestling match between Birkin and Gerald in which the idea of sex between them is expressed only in repression. It is a powerfully erotic scene. In it we see Birkin's bisexual nature struggling to express itself. It fails and that failure becomes the basis for the success of the film's idea.

When attempting to deal with bisexual reality in another novel, *The Fox*, Lawrence, it seems to me, fails the idea by creating a bisexual female whose end is tragic because she considers herself a failure in love. The bisexual is often portrayed directly as such in novels, films, and plays–and moreover, and regardless of story plausibility, as mean, neurotic, destructive, shallow, haunted, lying, two-faced, and at times not as bisexual at all but homosexual, with all of the negative characteristics society attributes to that condition.

With rare exceptions, then, the bisexual in action, when portrayed at all, is seen negatively. Appendix A, delineates a number of story lines and analyzes in detail how our culture views bisexual "reality."

Table I, below, lists the works covered in the appendix and indicates how the bisexual is seen.

Table I

Work	*Form*	*Bisexual Treatment*
1. *The Fox*	Novel Film	Ellen–ambivalent, a failure, the cause of her lover's death
2. *Giovanni's Room*	Novel	a. David–vacillating, weak, neurotic b. Giovanni–a villain, a killer, punished by death
3. "The Sea Change"	Short Story	Female lover–untrustworthy, hurts the one she loves
4. *Sunday Bloody Sunday*	Film	Bob–cannot love deeply, hurts the ones he loves
5. *Advise and Consent*	Novel	Senator Anderson–is blackmailed, commits suicide

6. *Butley*	Play Film	Butley–uncommitted, is hurt, and is an emotional failure
7. *Death in Venice*	Film	Aschenbach–a heterosexual cripple and failure
8. *The Front Runner*	Novel	Harlan Brown–seen as a homosexual
9. *The War Widow*	TV Play	Amy–seen as a lesbian
10. *Dog Day Afternoon*	Film	Sonny–a real bisexual portrayed realistically
11. *Portrait of a Marriage*	Biography	Vita and Harold Nicolson –a real bisexual couple portrayed realistically
12. *Teorema*	Film	Bisexual young man seen as a symbol
13. *Face to Face*	Film	Thomas–a bisexual seen as a symbol
14. *Gemini*	Play	Francis–a bisexual treated sympathetically and in a positive light
15. *The Shadow Box*	Play	Brian–bisexuality not as issue but a given fact

Thomas Geller's *Bisexuality: A Reader and Sourcebook* (1990) has a list of some other films and plays from around the world that deal with bisexuality.

It seems clear, then, that when the arts treat bisexuality truthfully, with balance, they do so on the more abstract level of *idea* than in the realistic or pseudorealistic depiction of characters and events.

In *Orlando*, for example, Virginia Woolf assumes the role of biographer to create a rich allegory for the union of the male and female principles in each individual. Because the story works on the level of fantasy, the transformation of the young nobleman Orlando into the noblewoman Orlando appears natural, acceptable. (For a detailed analysis of Woolf's treatment of the bisexual "idea," see Appendix A, p. 182. Despite its imaginative play with gender and time, *Orlando* portrays a recognizable world inhabited by people whose first question on the birth of a newborn baby is the perennial one. Orlando's change from man to woman is sequential: once the change is complete, he remains a she and is referred to by others as a woman. Woolf never suggests that Orlando can change back into a man, or back and forth, at will. Furthermore, Orlando is forced to play a conventional male role while a man and a conventional female role while a woman. In his/her world, the permeability of the gender barrier is severely limited: it is only breached the one time. And it is like our world insofar as what is masculine is seen as strong and protective, what is feminine is seen as weak and in need of protection. An in such a world pure respect for the human being as human being is at best difficult.

For a glimpse of a society where people are more than "man" or "woman," where indeed the mother of several children may be the father of several more, we have to go to another world–as Ursula K. LeGuin did in her award-winning science fiction novel, *The Left Hand of Darkness*.

The bisexual idea in *The Left Hand of Darkness* (a summary of the story line and its relation to bisexuality is found in Appendix A, p. 185) lies in the contrast it draws with the sexual dualism that pervades thinking in our own world, where men and women play the assigned male and female roles from birth. This includes the bisexual, who also on meeting another person casts him or her in the role of Man or Woman while him/herself adopting one or the other preset role. Were the roles not so rigid, we might find ourselves in a world with more room for true humanity, for people to grow, change, explore themselves and others.

That is, after all, what bisexuality is: simply another dimension of sexuality itself. Its only true distinction from the other sexualities is that the bisexual eroticizes both genders. In works of fantasy, such as *Orlando* and *The Left Hand of Darkness,* the bisexual idea can sometimes soar. In reality our sexual repressions are still very much with us–and the reality does carry over into artistic representations. Even in the hands of artists of genius, the bisexual often remains fenced in.

In *Women in Love*, the characters of Birkin, Ursula, Gerald, and Gudrun are set against the small colliery town in the midlands of England called Beldover. They are flesh-and-blood people living in the very real world of unrelenting Victorian repression. To all external appearances, they are heterosexual: Birkin is paired off with Ursula, and Gerald with Gudrun. Yet Lawrence develops between the two men a mutual ache for each other that is expressed in sometimes oblique, sometimes direct, but always close embroilment.

Consider this scene during a wedding party, in which Lawrence shows two men drawn together inexorably as though by the very tension between their irreconcilable values:

"You don't believe in having any standard of behavior at all, do you?" he challenged Birkin, censoriously.

"Standard–no. I hate standards. But they're necessary for the common ruck. Anybody who is anything can just be himself and do as he likes."

"But what do you mean by being himself?" said Gerald. "Is that an aphorism or a cliché?"

"I mean just doing what you want to do. I think it was perfect good form in Laura to bolt from Lupton to the church door. It was almost a masterpiece in good form. It's the hardest thing in the world to act spontaneously on one's impulses–and it's the only really gentlemanly thing to do–provided you're fit to do it."

"You don't expect me to take you seriously, do you?" asked Gerald.

"Yes, Gerald, you're one of the very few people I do expect that of."

"Then I'm afraid I can't come up to your expectations here, at any rate. You think people should just do as they like."

"I think they always do. But I should like them to like the purely individual thing in themselves, which makes them act in singleness. And they only like to do the collective thing."

"And I," said Gerald grimly, "shouldn't like to be in a world of people who acted individually and spontaneously, as you call it. We should have everybody cutting everybody else's throat in five minutes."....

There was a pause of strange enmity between the two men, that was very near to love. It was always the same between them; always their talk brought them into a deadly nearness of contact, a strange, perilous intimacy which was either hate or love, or both. They parted with apparent unconcern, as if their going apart were a trivial occurrence. Yet the heart of each burned from the other. They burned with each other, inwardly. This they would never admit. They intended to keep their relationship a casual free-and-easy friendship, they were not going to be so unmanly and unnatural as to allow any heart-burning between them. They had not the faintest belief in deep relationship between men and men, and their disbelief prevented any development of their powerful but suppressed friendliness.

Gerald and Birkin are intensely interested in the women in their lives, both emotionally and sexually. Lawrence in no way suggests that these men are repressing a desire for an *exclusive* relationship with each other. They are not closet homosexuals. Their problem is more complex than that. And yet it is simple. They love each other, and Lawrence wishes they could express that love openly. Yet he is too honest a writer to cause something to happen that *cannot* happen, given the era, the place, and the characters involved. And so the sexual tension between the two men is strong, if camouflaged.

"Gerald," he said, "I rather hate you."
"I know you do," said Gerald. "Why do you?"
Birkin mused inscrutably for some minutes.
"I should like to know if you are conscious of hating me," he said at last. "Do you ever consciously detest me–hate me with mystic hate? There are odd moments when I hate you starrily."
Gerald was rather taken aback, even a little disconcerted. He did not quite know what to say.
"I may, of course, hate you sometimes," he said. "But I'm not aware of it–never acutely aware of it, that is."
"So much the worse, is it?" he repeated.

There was a silence between the two men for some time, as the train ran on. In Birkin's face was a little irritable tension, a sharp knitting of the brows, keen and difficult. Gerald watched him warily, carefully, rather calculatingly, for he could not decide what he was after.

During a winter trip to the continent, Gerald dies, an apparent suicide. No one is as touched by Gerald's death as Birkin. He says to Ursula:

> "He should have loved me. I offered him."
> She, afraid, white, with mute lips, answered: "What difference would it have made!"
> "It would!" he said. "It would!"

Gerald's doom is sealed by Lawrence in an earlier scene. In it Birkin (Rupert) tries to reach into his friend and fails.

> "You've got to take down the love-and-marriage ideal from its pedestal. We want something broader. I believe in the *additional* perfect relationship between man and man–additional to marriage."
> "I can never see how they can be the same," said Gerald.
> "Not the same–but equally important, equally creative, equally sacred, if you like."
> "I know," said Gerald, "you believe something like that. Only I can't *feel* it, you see." He put his hand on Birkin's arm, with a sort of deprecating affection. And he smiled as if triumphantly.
> He was ready to be doomed. Marriage was like a doom to him. He was willing to condemn himself in marriage, to become like a convict condemned to the mines of the underworld, living no life in the sun, but having a dreadful subterranean activity. He was willing to accept this. And marriage was the seal of his condemnation. He was willing to be sealed thus in the underworld, like a soul damned but living for ever in damnation. But he would not make any pure relationship with any other soul. He could not. Marriage was not the committing of himself into a relationship with Gudrun. It was a commit-

ting of himself in acceptance of the established world, he would accept the established order, in which he did not livingly believe, and then he would retreat to the underworld for his life. This he would do.

The other way was to accept Rupert's offer of alliance, to enter into the bond of pure trust and love with the other man, and then subsequently with the woman. If he pledged himself with the man he would later be able to pledge himself with the woman: not merely in legal marriage, but in absolute, mystic marriage.

So Lawrence's bisexual idea remains that. An idea. An important, perhaps even profound, idea waiting for its time. Waiting for "reality," for people, for events to catch up.

Ursula tells Birkin he cannot have two kinds of love because it's false and impossible.

"I don't believe that," he answers.

Neither do I.

Chapter 10

The Bisexual Future: Present-Day Factors

So far we have looked at bisexuality as it has been and as it is now. The temptation in any conclusion is to crane the neck around a distant corner to bring a view of what will be. I'm afraid, though, that to claim such foresight would be presumptuous. I don't know what will be–no one does. Obviously, though, the present affects the future just as the past has affected the present. There are dynamics at work that will shape things to come. If we cannot foretell the bisexual future through these present factors, we can list and break them down, in a spirit of inquiry rather than prophecy.

There are, it seems to me, nine major factors in the present that will probably affect bisexuals in the future.

AIDS. In the 1980s the AIDS epidemic spread like wildfire through the two populations of male gays and IV drug users. Of course this scourge deeply affected the bisexual population as well. Already in 1983 the Bisexual Forum in New York had its first member die of AIDS.

Early in the 1990s, the world's medical and scientific experts are extensively investigating the bisexual population in order to find out how many people are at risk, who they are, and how to reach them. For all the reasons mentioned above in the section on sociological studies, they are finding out just how difficult it is to get accurate and meaningful statistics.

At first the self-identified bisexual community ran for cover. I know of many bisexual men who became practicing heterosexuals. Former "swingers" decided to become monogamous and quite a number of bisexual women eliminated many if not all male partners.

As knowledge of the importance of practicing safe sex has spread, and as the epidemic has raged on year after year, the sexual behavior of the bisexual has indeed changed, just as has that of the male gay population. There are now more monogamous relationships and fewer indiscriminate sexual liaisons among people who define themselves as bisexual.

The main problem however, is that the bisexual identity is just one variable in a person's orientation. Too easily overlooked are all those people who practice bisexual behavior but call themselves heterosexual, and members of communities, such as the African-American or Latino communities, in whose cultures bisexual behavior is viewed in an extremely negative light, and whom education on safe sex still often fails to reach.

The bisexual is indeed caught in this devastating epidemic. Bisexual men, just like gay men, are at risk, as are their women partners, whether bisexual or heterosexual. More and more women are being infected with the virus. The bisexual is, alas, one conduit of AIDS between the heterosexual and homosexual communities spreading the disease from one section of the population to the other. Hopefully before too long, a cure and/or vaccine will be discovered and this deadly factor in the life of the bisexual, the homosexual, and the heterosexual will be eradicated.

Sex Roles and Stereotypes. Who is masculine? Who is feminine? In Queen Victoria's time these were not questions but assumptions. They are assumptions still, but not to the same rigid degree. Although many still accept without question that what is male is "masculine" and what is female is "feminine," we live in a world more open to individual choice. It is becoming more and more clear that such answers do not reflect a law of nature, but imposed cultural attitudes. Assumptions, however, die hard.

The era in which people passively accepted simplistic male and female stereotypes, and embraced the false security inherent in assigned sex roles, is ending. Truth is indeed setting us free–to see, for example, that in one culture (our own) aggressiveness is considered an essentially masculine trait, in another (Tchambuli), a feminine trait, in a third (Munduguma) both a masculine and a feminine trait, and a fourth (Arapesh) a trait shunned by both sexes. This is not to say that there are not biological, as well as cultural, differences between what men and women think and how they behave. But the two sexes share more similarities than differences. What makes this obvious truth difficult to absorb culturally is that we surround the physiological differences with marketable symbols, such as lipstick and dresses for women, neckties, sporting goods and hunting weapons for men. These symbols have nothing intrinsically to do with men and women as they really are, but everything to do with how we want them to be.

Cultural stereotypes of masculinity and femininity are changing all the time. Yes, there are differences between what men and women think and how they behave; but any given list of these differences is merely a list of gender characteristics in a particular culture at a specific time.

George Washington wore a wig and ruffles. In World War II "Rosie the Riveter" emerged as a national symbol of femininity by holding down a man's job. Rosie was a wartime necessity, albeit one her grandmother would probably not have understood.

But in a very real sense Rosie, a creation of American wartime propaganda, freed American women from the stereotypical, centuries-old idea of what a woman is made for. After the war, the housewife-and-mother ideal was reimposed and remained more or less in force for 20 more years. But Rosie was resurrected in the political ferment of the 1960s and the women's movement. And now the raised consciousness of women is forcing change in what is expected of both sexes. Women have had to carry the burden of such characterizations as "hysterical," "passive," "frivolous," etcetera. The male-ideal counterparts of these clichés are enumerated by Deborah S. David and Robert Brannon in *The Forty-Nine Percent Majority* as follows:

1. No Sissy Stuff: The stigma of all stereotyped feminine characteristics and qualities, including openness and vulnerability;
2. The Big Wheel: Success, status, and the need to be looked up to;
3. The Sturdy Oak: A manly air of toughness, confidence, and self-reliance;
4. Give 'Em Hell: The aura of aggression, violence, and daring.

But these stereotypes, thanks largely to the women's movement, have begun to change rapidly. New words have come into general use. "Fathering" is one. It expresses the idea that fathering a child is not the same thing as merely being the father. Fathering, like

mothering, bespeaks a care and devotion beyond what has previously been expected of fathers. This development promises exciting
possibilities for the future.

Old norms are changing with respect to sex itself. "Open marriage" and "swinging" have been around and accepted by some
people as a way of life for over 20 years. However, with the advent
of AIDS in the 1980s, these lifestyles have once again been put on
the cultural back burner. Homosexuality has gained widespread
acceptance in the medical, psychological, and social science fields,
largely through the efforts of the homosexual community itself.
Because these changes tell us that the sex roles of men and women
are not as inflexible as they were before, we have to conclude that
the bisexual, too, is having an easier time. It is allowable now for
men to be more emotional, more caring, even more passive if passivity is appropriate and needed. Women can be strong, assertive,
dominant, even tough, if they choose. The male's passivity can be
expressed with both men and women; and the female can be more
assertive toward both sexes, too. Where will all this lead the bisexual? It should, minimally, make the road he or she travels smoother,
less an uphill struggle than before. In a word–progress.

Androgyny. Of all the factors affecting the future of bisexuality,
androgyny (the internal and/or external appearance of male and
female characteristics in one person) is the most obscure because its
core rests firmly in paradox. As Freud wrote:

> . . . all human individuals as a result of their bisexual disposi-
> tion and of cross-inheritance, combine in themselves both
> masculine and feminine characteristics so that pure masculin-
> ity and femininity remain theoretical constructions of uncer-
> tain content (1925, *SE*, XIX, p. 258).

Freud is not commenting on androgyny directly, but he builds a
case for its existence nonetheless. Androgyny has been represented
for ages in various philosophies and myths. For example, the Tao
concept of Yang and Yin combines in one the dualities of light and
darkness, masculine and feminine; it teaches that if lovers are to
become one each must seek within himself or herself the opposite
principle. A woman must find the man in her being and a man must

find the woman in his before they can truly understand each other and become one.

Androgyny is often confused with bisexuality, hermaphroditism, and even homosexuality. It is none of these things. It is the recognizing of polarities, the accepting of paradoxes and apparent contradictions. It is feeling united while at the same time feeling separate. In *Androgyny*, Dr. June Singer says, "Androgyny refers to a specific way of joining the 'masculine' and 'feminine' aspects of a single human being" Jung's anima and animus apply as well to the internal female and male characteristics in all human beings.

Bisexuality, on the other hand, is the external sexual manifestation of the duality of maleness and femaleness: the attraction to both sexes. An androgynous person need not be bisexual, and a bisexual need not be androgynous. But androgyny is nevertheless a word to reckon with when considering the future of bisexuality, first because it has become a more familiar (and less frightening) archetype in popular consciousness and culture, and second because, conjoined with androgyny, bisexuality becomes the unification of dual attractions. Obviously the more we recognize the androgynous aspects of our being, the better we understand and more intimately we can relate to each other, within and across gender boundaries.

There is every reason to believe that with the changes in sex roles and sex stereotypes discussed earlier, androgyny in all its meaning, both real and mythical, will find a more than marginal place in the collective consciousness of the future, and this consciousness will undoubtedly change the way we view sexuality in general and bisexuality in particular.

Friendship, Lovers–and Bisexuality. With the possible exception of work, nothing in life pulls us together or tears us apart like the bonding we experience with friends and lovers. The condition of being "in love" has a standing in our consciousness higher than friendship and the love shared between friends. Only in our literature and movies do we place friends on as high a plane as lovers. Huckleberry Finn and Jim, Butch Cassidy and the Sundance Kid, and Thelma and Louise provide examples of friendship on a scale as moving in their fashion as the love relationships in *Romeo and Juliet* and *Anna Karenina*.

Some feel the highest compliment a man can give his wife is to acknowledge that she is not only a wonderful wife but also his best friend. When attempting to combine friendship with sex, however, trouble develops more often than not. When two people share sex as part of a larger relationship, a complex and mysterious game begins, having to do with power and the struggle for a dominant position. This struggle exists in friendship, too, but it can be played out in such areas as sports, hobbies, and business. Lovers need not necessarily share anything except love. They express that feeling through sex, which fills the space that friends must fill with what they share in common. This is not to say that there are no people who do not share both sex and friendship, but the combination is difficult to maintain because we tend to view the love relationship as a condition of automatic pleasure. But love, whether between friends, lovers, or both, is work–good work. To have a lover who is a friend as well is twice the pleasure, requiring and deserving twice the work.

Something we don't always demand in a lover but do in a friend is trust. Alas, this is realized more consistently in fictional friendships than in factual ones. Perhaps we idealize friendship so because we need to believe in the trust of friends–of Huck and Jim, Butch and Sundance–more than in that of lovers. Of lovers we expect the heat of sexuality with all its volatility, its potential to turn to hate, even violence. We expect of friends that they will go on floating down the Mississippi forever, on an endless river of friendship.

Still, power struggles do not keep people from making friends and lovers and keeping them for long periods. With heterosexuals the problem of sex in friendship does not appear often because heterosexual men and women are not encouraged to view each other apart from their sexual differences. Generally, heterosexuals' best friends are of the same gender while homosexuals' best friends are most often of the opposite sex. Bisexuals must constantly deal with possible sexual attraction in friendship. They must settle the problem of sexual arousal by self-imposed restrictions since they do not live in the simpler world of one-gender choice that the heterosexual and homosexual find so comfortable.

As one bisexual said: "It's great to be able to make it in bed with my friends *if we so desire.*" If they do not "so desire," there is no problem. But self-imposed restrictions keep the doors of change constantly swinging. The aware bisexual knows that desire cannot always be so easily regulated, and that the friend who holds no sexual attraction today could tomorrow. The heterosexual and homosexual take their fixed place in the sexual spectrum more for granted. The bisexual's equilibrium is not so easily fixed.

The aware bisexual, looking for present-day factors that will affect his or her future in friendship or love, would not seem to have a great deal to go on. Yet more and more people are giving to their sexuality a place equal to what has always been given to basic needs such as food, shelter, and sleep. In the past, women were encouraged to be suspicious of one another, causing most women to find it nearly impossible to bond in friendship the way men do. These two factors alone, the recognition of sexuality as a necessary and healthy human need and the readier bonding between women, will undoubtedly bring enormous changes in how we view the bisexual and how the bisexual views him- or herself.

The Family. A woman at a recent dinner party spoke to me of the bisexual lifestyle and how it is becoming more popular. What she meant by "bisexual life-style" was the person who lives by him- or herself and has sex with both genders—a man on one night, a woman on another. But, as we've seen, there is no one lifestyle when we speak of the bisexual. The arch of behavior is wide and the avenue of expression broad. A bisexual lifestyle can even be satisfactorily expressed through a family, children, and one or two close friends. It can be expressed in a single relationship with a member of one sex, or in a couple of relationships with members of either or both sexes. The bisexual life can also be lived in sequential monogamous relationships or in "open marriage."

The family as such is very much involved when bisexuality is considered. What family factors today concern the bisexual in the future? Many. Let me mention some of the more important ones.

1. Divorce rates keep rising in the U.S. year after year.
2. The number of divorced people under the age of 35 is over 80 per 1000 married persons.
3. More and more people are living alone.
4. The number of single-parent families has skyrocketed.

Other factors include the increase in the number of working women and their resulting financial independence; and greater mobility in our civilization, which is also loosening family ties–if not those of the nuclear, then those of the extended family of uncles, aunts, cousins, and even brothers and sisters when they become adults and move away. Other options become, available, other methods of close relationships must be formed.

The monogamous ideal of the past is being seriously questioned in all parts of society, which encourages the bisexual to speak out. In a discussion at the Bisexual Forum held in March 1977, of 17 people present, not one believed in monogamy for him/herself at the current time. Three people desired it for the future but not for then. One happily married man, who came closest to it by being monogamous with his wife for 23 years of marriage, had only one male lover friend at any one time and only a total of three while married. A number of married and formerly married men and women had been monogamous for periods of one to ten years but none were currently monogamous. Most desired open relationships with one primary partner. The general consensus was that no one person could fulfill all the emotional and sexual needs of a person and that other people were desirable and even necessary.

Nothing else in bisexuality is more historically important than this simple "truth": what was once both religious and civil law–one man, one woman, one lifetime–is now in question. Millions of people who half a generation ago embraced a monogamous lifestyle–venturing outside it only in secret–are attending a new sociological god, autonomy, whereby, whether in a true or illusory spirit of freedom, one is open to self-exploration through emotional and sexual relatedness with more than one person in a lifetime and, for many, more than one person at a time.

However, in the last ten years, with the epidemic of AIDS, this practice of sexual relations with more than one person at a time has been diminished to a great extent. Some bisexuals practice monogamy where previously they were "swingers," some have decided to have many fewer contacts outside their prime relationship, and those who have continued their former open lifestyle are now carefully practicing safe sex.

"Lesbian, Gay & BiEqual Rights and Liberation movement." In April 1977, the White House invited the National Gay Task Force to hear its views on discrimination against homosexuals. This extraordinary event occurred only eight years after the Stonewall riots in 1969, in which hundreds of gays clashed with New York City police over the question of police brutality during a raid on a gay bar.

This outstretched hand from the Executive Branch also held out the promise of a new outlook toward bisexuals. In the mind of the general public, the homosexual and the bisexual are synonymous. If the men and women privy to the most powerful office on earth were willing to listen, who knew what changes the future might hold in store? Though the more recent Republican administrations of Reagan and Bush have proved rather less sympathetic to their non-heterosexual constituencies, the new Clinton presidency is once more listening to these minority groups. Though the extreme religious right tries to outlaw and circumscribe gays and lesbians, the gays and lesbians themselves continue to flex their political muscle, adding more cities and states that have passed anti-sexual orientation ordinances. Thus, as gays build a higher self-image, the bisexual, too, may begin to occupy a more firmly rooted place in society.

The Women's Movement and Feminism. The women's movement, awakening as it did in 1968 from the half-sleep it entered after women got the vote in 1920, has unalterably changed American life. It is all but impossible to imagine what American culture was like without it.

Like all movements, this one has its factions, and an important one is its own gay population. In the past, *male* homosexuality was more or less the condition people thought of when they thought of homosexuality at all. As with most other things, homosexuality was very much a "man's world." But ideas of what is a man and woman are changing, and these ideas will undoubtedly help to make it a *people's* world. In this world, the lesbian will hold a place in our culture equal to that of the male homosexual. From that position she affects the consciousness of *all* women, who will thus be more likely to confront their possible homosexual component–and be tolerated and, one hopes, respected for it.

Feminism, with its emphasis on the latent power inherent in what is female, tends to make it more acceptable for men to acknowledge that part of themselves. Men can be less concerned with the problem of establishing their manliness, thereby helping to free both themselves and women to more fully explore their sexual natures.

Women have thrown off for good the cliché images of powder-puff simplemindedness and passivity. A happy fallout is that men can express what is *womanly* within them with less fear of social opprobrium. And as men in turn free themselves of old-time clichés of machoism, it becomes more acceptable for women to express what is *manly* about them.

Whatever was female was long considered inferior. One of the most insidious results of such downgrading of half the human race was the mistrust and alienation it caused among women themselves. While men could form bonds of mutual respect for one another, women could not; they were taught not to respect themselves. Today, women have new respect for themselves and therefore for other women. They are able to see bisexuality as *one* of the roads leading to a closer bond between women. This is bound to lead to a more understanding and tolerant attitude toward bisexuality in the future.

This change is already evident by the overwhelming adoption of a Sexual Orientation declaration by the 1977 National Womens' Conference held in Houston. In 1992, Elizabeth Reba Weise edited an anthology of writings by 21 women on the topic of feminism and bisexuality, *Closer to Home, Bisexuality and Feminism.*

This new-found strength has also changed the bisexual movement to a large extent. In the past five years many bisexual women in the lesbian community have decided to counter the prejudice of many lesbians towards themselves by breaking away from the lesbian community and forming new bisexual organizations. Some of these new organizations have continued to have only female members while others have opened their associations to men. The result is that there are now over 50 bisexual organizations in the U.S.

The first National Bisexual Conference, held in San Francisco in the middle of 1990, was an example of the role of the female bisexual. It was through the energy and drive of the women organizers that it took place. There is available now an International Directory of Bisexual Groups. (For a current copy of the most recent Directory, you can send a self-addressed stamped envelope and a donation of $2.00 to: Robyn Ochs, East Coast Bisexual Network, c/o GLSC, 338 Newbury St., Boston, MA 02115.)

In addition, there now seems to be a sufficient number of organizations in the Western world that permit a beginning trend of bisexual conferences meeting on an international level. The United Kingdom put on its tenth National Conference in 1992. In 1991 Amsterdam hosted successfully the First International Bisexual Conference where 200 participants from ten countries gathered. London hosted the Second International Bisexual Conference in October of 1992, and New York is planning to host the Third International Conference in 1994 in conjunction with the 25th anniversary of the Stonewall Riots.

Myths. Misinformation and lack of information about bisexuality is very much what this book is about. There follows a simple list of the myths surrounding bisexuality in two broad categories: the myth of nonexistence, and the myth of neurosis, both of which will play an important role in the shaping of the bisexual future.

Nonexistence Myth	*Neurotic Myth*
1. A person is *either* straight *or* gay.	1. The bisexual is by definition neurotic.
2. There is no such entity as bisexuality.	2. The bisexual cannot love deeply.
3. The bisexual is really a homosexual.	3. The bisexual is mixed up and can't make up his/her mind.
4. Bisexuality is only a transition stage.	4. The bisexual is hyper-sexed and sex crazy.

Dilemmas. The bisexual's dilemma is twofold: his/her interaction with society on the one hand, and his/her internal problem on the other. Until now, the overwhelming social attitude toward the bisexual has been one of denial. This is a classic attitude of large groups of people toward anyone different. But how different are bisexuals? Now many people, some of them famous, are broadcasting their bisexual natures. Many people are illuminating what we now know to be bisexual behavior. The door to the closet will never close so firmly again.

If bisexuals are a problem to others, the others are even more of a dilemma to bisexuals. And the bisexuals themselves are the ones who live with the condition. Both groups of people should profit from better understanding in the future. To understand the bisexual is to understand ourselves better, no matter what our sexual orientation. And with understanding comes growth–as individuals and as a society. Again, in a word–progress.

Sex. What a powerful three-letter word. What a joy. What a burden. After millions of years of living with it, we are as awed and as baffled by its power as we are by the meaning of life itself. If we are ever to learn the truth of that meaning, the understanding of sex will be an essential key to the mystery. Millenniums have passed in darkness. The future–for people of all varieties on the spectrum of sexual orientation–looks brighter.

Bisexuality is now staking its claim upon our serious consideration as a real force for bringing about that brighter future.

Such, at least, is the premise of this book.

APPENDIX A

The Bisexual as Portrayed in the Arts

THE "REALITY"

1. The Fox

> . . . It had seemed so easy to make one beloved creature happy. And the more you tried, the worse the failure. It was terrible. She had been all her life reaching, reaching, and what she reached for seemed so near, until she had stretched to her utmost limit. And then it was always beyond her. . . . She was glad Jill was dead for she had realized that she could never make her happy.

These are the thoughts and feelings of Ellen March at the end of D. H. Lawrence's novella, *The Fox*. Written in 1923, *The Fox* is a haunting story of two women and a man entangled in a web of unhappy love. The two women have a difficult time making a go of their farm. Jill Banford, the principal investor, is "a small, thin, delicate thing with spectacles." Ellen is the "man" about the place. She does four-fifths of the work. These 30-year-old, spinsterish, educated women are "attached to each other." One day Henry, a 20-year-old soldier, appears. He reminds Ellen of the fox that has been preying on the chicken coop. Though exasperated by the animal, she is also mesmerized by it and cannot force herself to kill it. Within a short time, Henry asks Ellen to marry him–and kills the fox. Ellen is caught between the love of Jill and the love of Henry. She vacillates, unable to make a decision. But the decision is taken out of Ellen's hands when Jill is killed by the falling tree that Henry cuts down.

Writing in the 1920s, Lawrence was not explicit regarding the sexual behavior of the characters involved. However, Ellen's bisexuality and Jill's lesbianism are clearly inferred through their emotional ties, their declarations of need and love, and by the fact that they sleep in the same bed. Ellen's involvement with the man is more explicit; she marries him after Jill's death. But at no time did Lawrence describe sexual involvement between the man and woman apart from one kiss before their marriage.

In 1968 the novella was made into a film, with Anne Heywood playing Ellen; Sandy Dennis, Jill; and Keir Dullea, Henry. Two generations after the novella was first published, sexual explicitness was taken for granted, and what was only implied in the book is shown cinematically in graphic detail. We see Ellen masturbating in front of a mirror, enjoying heterosexual fantasies. The two women make love in their bedroom. Henry and Ellen have a love scene in an abandoned cabin.

In the novella Ellen is ambivalent in her desires, and though seen as strong in a number of respects–especially in her relationship with Jill–she ends up as a passive, unhappy, and self-acknowledged failure. But the negative aspect of bisexuality is strongly emphasized when her indecision concerning her sexuality is followed by her death. Bisexuality is seen as an ambiguous state that cannot survive. A choice has to be made–give up either the male or female sexual object, and its corollary, relinquish the inner woman or man. Either-or. Ellen could not kill the fox, the male symbol. But the female object was killed and thereby Ellen's inner masculinity. Ellen allowed it to happen. "And she–she wanted to sit still, like a woman on the last milestone, and watch." Yet she could not submit, could not surrender her inner androgynous self. Though her husband wished it, she did not "have all her own life as a woman and a female," but still was "a man, a woman with a man's responsibility."

Reviews of the film (with a notable exception by Judith Crist) do not refer to bisexuality, though they provide a synopsis of the plot. Lesbianism, however, is mentioned in relation to the two women. So, although there are only three characters, it is the bisexual one who does not exist. The critic who mentioned bisexuality said this:

> . . . but Anne Heywood, who plays the girl who is desired by both male and female, is sheer perfection in a stunning por-

trayal of a woman *torn by the bisexuality that obsesses us all.*
[Author's italics]

2. Giovanni's Room

D. H. Lawrence's portrayal of Ellen as a self-admitted failure was mild compared to James Baldwin's delineation of bisexuals in his novel, *Giovanni's Room*. He treats the difficulty of love with an intensity that permits a glimpse into the internal private hell of the neurotic bisexual. And once again, as in *The Fox*, the bisexual is depicted as one who, directly or indirectly, kills.

Giovanni's Room is one of the very few mainstream novels with two bisexuals as the protagonists. David, a handsome, blond, young American living in France to "find himself," meets the dark and handsome Giovanni in a gay bar in Paris. The two men begin an affair that night, and David moves into Giovanni's small, dingy room. David, torn by guilty desire, finally leaves Giovanni to return to his fiancée Hella, who had been in Spain trying to decide whether or not to marry him. Down on his luck and without a job, Giovanni ends up killing his former employer. He is found guilty and guillotined. David's love for Hella turns sour, he loses her and turns to men again.

In fiction, the bisexual is more often than not depicted as the villain–the spy or the traitors–or the weak, vacillating neurotic. In *Giovanni's Room* both types are juxtaposed. Giovanni and David share one quality: both are outsiders, both foreign elements in their adopted society. Giovanni, the Italian, is the foreign worker who is looked down on by the French, yet doesn't fit his native Italian culture either, being unable to propagate his own kind (his baby was born "twisted, gray and dead"). David, the American expatriate, also feels alienated in France. He is neither in harmony with the homosexual world of Paris nor the heterosexual world of America. He belongs nowhere and to no one, not to Giovanni, not to Hella, and most important, not to himself. He remains a dim shadow, without substance.

Giovanni comes through the pages sharply molded, a real person, a man whose essence contains a major flaw. Giovanni is able to love: He loved his wife and he loved David. But Giovanni also kills. When his baby is born dead, he renounces his religion, his wife, his home and runs to Paris. In Paris he destroys not symbolically but actually. This in turn seals his doom and execution. The bisexual, it would seem, is not to be trusted. Destruction follows his footsteps in the heterosexual as well as in the homosexual world. And in the end he is destroyed.

David is not endowed with such epic qualities. His essence is riddled with personality defects and neurotic failings. He cannot love, cannot even get close. He hurts the people who love him–his family: his male lover Giovanni, and Hella, the woman in his life. He also hurts the peripheral people in his life: Joey, with whom as a teenager he has his first male sexual experience, is made unhappy because of David's guilt; Sue, a girl he uses to prove his manhood, is also manipulated. This inability to love is clearly voiced by Giovanni when David leaves him:

> "You are not leaving me for her," he said. "You are leaving me for some other reason. You lie so much, you have come to believe all your own lies. But I, I have senses. You are not leaving me for a woman. If you were really in love with this little girl, you would not have had to be so cruel to me . . . .
> "You do not," cried Giovanni, sitting up, "love anyone! You never have loved anyone. I am sure you never will! You love your purity, you love your mirror– . . . . And you–you are immoral. You are, by far, the most immoral man I have met in all my life. Look, *look* what you have done to me. Do you think you could have done this if I did not love you? Is this what you should do to love?"

David's bisexuality is not real. It is a transition to homosexuality, a way station, though it covers many years. It begins with his inclination toward homosexuality as a teenager. Then comes the repression, and running away.

> I had decided to allow no room in the universe for something which shamed and frightened me. I succeeded very well–by not looking at the universe, by not looking at myself, by remaining, in effect, in constant motion.

He becomes a lover who "is neither man nor woman," nothing that can be known or touched. His vacillating movements, his many women, and his "joyless seas of alcohol" were part of his unconscious homosexuality trying to get out. And in the end his bisexuality does evolve into homosexuality. Hella is discarded, "since all that once delighted him turned sour on his stomach." His "true" nature emerges as he goes off to Nice, roaming ". . . all the bars and at the end of the first night, blind with alcohol and grim with lust, [he] climbed the stairs of a dark hotel in company with a sailor."

3. *"The Sea Change"*

Baldwin's tragic image is perhaps the nadir of the bisexual's portrait. In most of the few cases where the bisexual is depicted at all, emerging from the world of nonexistence, violence and death are *not* shown to be the result. The pain the bisexual brings about is more often emotional than physical. In his short story "The Sea Change," Ernest Hemingway sketches such a scene. At the end of the summer, the handsome, tanned young couple are sitting in a Parisian cafe. He has just found out that she wants to go off with a woman. She tells him that he must understand that she loves him, he must let her go off; she will return to him. He understands, is hurt, but he lets her go. The action changes him, however, to the extent that he even looks different in the mirror. Once again the bisexual is someone who cannot be trusted, someone who is not loyal, and someone who cuts deeply into the lover's psyche.

4. *Sunday Bloody Sunday*

In *Sunday Bloody Sunday* the wounding of a loved one is exquisitely shown. Both Alex Grenville (Glenda Jackson) and Dr. Daniel Hirsh (Peter Finch) are emotionally hurt by Bob Elkin (Murray Head), their bisexual lover. Reviewers described this film as moving, adult, and wise–a movie that explored how people cope successfully with the pain of partial loves and terminated affairs. The two main characters are fully realized. Alex is a 34-year-old, bright, educated divorceé. Daniel, a Jewish doctor in his early forties, successful, urbane, cultivated, and sensitive, is homosexual but thoroughly masculine. The film depicts the last week of their parallel love affairs with Bob, 25, the kinetic sculptor emerging from the lower class, who in a cowardly fashion leaves both of them and London for a new life in the States.

The characters do not have guilt and self-pity because of their sexual orientation. As John Schlesinger, the director, said in an interview:

> The doctor *happened* to be homosexual, but that was not the point of the film. The woman *happened* to have been married before, but that was not the point of the film. The boy *happened* to enjoy being with both of them, but the picture is not trying to explain his bisexuality. His bisexuality is a fact.

And to that extent the movie is highly successful.

Bob's bisexuality is a fact. But how is he depicted as a human being? As a bisexual how does he affect events? Here we perceive once again the blurred negative image of the bisexual. When I left the theater, I asked myself what these two highly intelligent and sensitive people could see in Bob, the object of their love. I was not alone in asking this question. Here are some descriptions of Bob from the critics: "shallow," "doesn't know how to give of himself," "callous and callow," "a free spirit not yet formed with access to everything," "a mere type," "nothing in him is revealed except perhaps youth and cockiness and *nostalgie de la boue*," "elusive," "having the new morality of enlightened selfishness," "conveys a passivity and deficiency of feeling that hardly recommends him as a love object," and "on a lower rung of the evolutionary ladder."

The bisexual is envisioned and portrayed as a human being whose bisexuality is symptomatic of his inability to love deeply and who must, because of his sexual orientation, hurt those who love him. Bob says of himself: "I know you don't think you're getting enough of me, but you're getting all there is." And Alex replies: "Perhaps you shouldn't spread yourself so thin." The bisexual as emotional villain.

5. Advise and Consent

If the bisexual is seen as a person who hurts and wounds his or her loved ones, then it must follow that he or she would also be represented as being the injured one, the receiver of pain.

In Allen Drury's novel, *Advise and Consent*, Senator Brigham Anderson is a historical bisexual (played by Richard Kiley when it was adapted for the stage in 1960 and by Don Murray in its Otto Preminger movie treatment in 1962). Senator Anderson, a happily married man, is blackmailed over possible exposure of his past wartime homosexual experience. Here, the melodramatic solution to the bisexual's dilemma is death by his own hand. As in *Giovanni's Room*, this extreme resolution of the bisexual's problems is not typical. More often the bisexual is seen as being only emotionally hurt and psychologically wounded.

6. Butley

In Simon Gray's 1972 theater piece, Ben Butley is an example of a bisexual who is emotionally hurt. *Butley* was also filmed in 1974, with, as in the play, Alan Bates in the title role. Bates plays a London University English teacher who in the course of one day learns that his wife is finally leaving him for another man and that his young male lover is also opting for a new partner. In this day of personal failure we see Butley railing at his colleagues, loathing his students, and despising himself. Though charming and witty, he is portrayed as bitter, cruel, rude, and full of alcoholic self-pity. He is committed to nothing–not to love, not to friendship, not to his profession. He is unable to maintain satisfactory emotional involvements–either heterosexual or homosexual. Though he is extremely adept at verbal darts (some quite poisonous), it is Butley who is hurt, who aches emotionally and who suffers psychological pain.

7. Death in Venice

There is one aspect of fictional psychological failure that applies not only to the bisexual but to the homosexual as well. To some extent, the bisexual and homosexual are as they are because they are seen as failed heterosexuals being fixated in an early stage of psychosexual development. This idea is at the heart of the classical psychoanalytic explanation of any orientation other than heterosexuality. A perfect example is Luchino Visconti's 1971 film adaptation of Thomas Mann's classic novella, *Death in Venice*.

Though Mann's masterwork deals with the character of Aschenbach, aging, attracted to the elusive young Tadzio, it does not deal overtly with sex. It is the story of a decaying society and dying values. Visconti, however, turns *Death in Venice* into a sexual story. Aschenbach (married, the father of a daughter) is portrayed by Dirk Bogard, playing helpless counterpoint to the beautiful Tadzio's flirting eyelashes. To explain Aschenbach's behavior we are shown a scene (not in Mann's work) in which he is unable to function sexually with a woman. Of course, anyone can be neurotic; I have no argument with a bisexual being portrayed as a neurotic individual, but why must the bisexual *always* be seen that way?

Recently, the homosexual man and woman have achieved a considerable degree of acceptance in art and literature, as well as in society. The bisexual in this regard tends to ride on the homosexual's coattails. In the last couple of years, for example, a number of pieces have been written or produced in which the bisexual is treated as a homosexual, and as a homosexual is depicted positively. The progress is slow . . . but it is progress.

8. The Front Runner

The Front Runner, a novel by Patricia Nell Warren published in 1974, shows the bisexual as a homosexual. Harlan Brown, a 39-year-old track coach, falls in love with his star runner, Billy Sive. The novel explores their loving relationship. In this tragic story the homosexual is seen as real and human. As homosexual, both lovers are depicted in a positive light. But Harlan Brown's homosexuality is emphasized, and his bisexuality is all but ignored. He is depicted as homosexual in many respects: he views himself as such, he prefers men erotically and emotionally, he lived in the gay subculture for a number of years. His relations with women, on the other hand, are less important–casual sexual alliances in high school and a bad marriage that produced two children and ended in divorce. As a homosexual Harlan Brown is depicted sympathetically; his bisexuality is relegated to the realm of near nonexistence.

9. The War Widow

Lesbian love also has begun to receive some kind treatment. In the fall of 1976, Harvey Perr's original TV script, *The War Widow*, was presented on the PBS series "Visions." It is the tender story of two women, Amy and Jenny. World War I finds Amy's husband away in France at the Front. Amy does not feel the separation, or for that matter much else. But her world begins to brighten when she meets Jenny, a photographer. She falls in love with Jenny. In the end, she makes the difficult choice of leaving her past life to live with her loved one. Once again we have the rich, full portrayal of two homosexual people. What is excluded is Amy's bisexuality. It is there, but it is vague, it is not dealt with, it is ignored. Amy would seem to be a lesbian, her marriage a sham. As a lesbian she is understood and viewed with sympathy. As a bisexual her existence is fuzzy.

It is where documentary reality impinges that the bisexual does seem to be finally recognized. The two stand-out examples are the film *Dog Day Afternoon* and Nigel Nicolson's biography of his parents, *Portrait of a Marriage*.

10. Dog Day Afternoon

The character of Sonny in Sidney Lumet's 1975 film, *Dog Day Afternoon*, is based on Littlejohn Basso, the bisexual bank robber who was sentenced to serve 20 years in the penitentiary. The movie is based on his actual Brooklyn robbery attempt in 1972. Holding nine hostages in the bank for 14 hours, he became an instant celebrity, seen by millions as he starred in a live, televised robbery-in-progress. His motivation? He needed money for his boyfriend's (to whom he was "married") sex-change operation. The film portrays this bisexual realistically. He is a bank robber, he has a wife and children whom he loves, and he is deeply involved with a male transsexual. What we see is a likable, neurotic, tenderhearted loser in over his head, dominated by forces both internal and external over which he has little control. His bisexuality is a fact and is portrayed as such. This outrageous bank robber was treated true to life; of course, in his case the truth teetered on the edge of bizarre, fantastical fiction–which may have helped.

11. Portrait of a Marriage

A different kind of bisexual reality comes through in the book *Portrait of a Marriage*, in which Nigel Nicolson describes the bisexual "truth" of the 49-year marriage of his parents, Vita and Harold, as "the strangest and most successful union that two gifted people have ever enjoyed." They were two bisexual English writers born into the upper class in the late nineteenth century. They brought to their marriage mutual esteem, intelligence, and a deep and lasting love, though they each had numerous involvements mainly "but not exclusively" with members of their own sex.

The major part of the book deals with the stormy period in 1918-20 precipitated by Vita's passionate love affair with Violet Trefusis. The crisis is resolved, Vita returns to her husband and home, and until her death in 1962 remains in a marriage that in her own words "included enthusiasm, deep love as well as commitment." Vita Sackville-West, as this novelist and poet was known, is portrayed well. She is shown with faults as well as virtues. She was headstrong, with the ability to be coldly indifferent, but also passionate and giving to those she loved. Though she was rather an aristocratic snob, she was nonetheless a rebel against the assigned female role of the period.

Harold Nicolson's contradictions are also delineated. We see a man who loves his wife deeply even while he has numerous affairs with young men. Though a racist, he felt deeply over the plight of the Jews under Hitler.

The Nicolsons did exist. Their bisexuality was a fact. But to call him feminine or her masculine would be absurd. That men and women possess many of the same traits and feel many of the same emotions is hardly a new idea today, but to see how two sensitive people lived this reality in post-Victorian England is eye-opening and exciting.

The portrayals of the bisexual in Paolo Pasolini's 1968 film *Teorema* and Ingmar Bergman's 1976 movie *Face to Face* lie between the negative "reality" and the idea of bisexual truth; both films deal with other matters, and use the bisexual as a symbol or example.

12. Teorema

This film is a parable. One day a beautiful young man mysteriously appears at the home of a wealthy Italian family. He proceeds to make love to the father, mother, son, daughter, and maid. When a telegram arrives and the young man must leave, all five members of the family are dramatically changed. The maid becomes a saint, performing miracles, the daughter turns catatonic, the son in ultimate absurdity urinates on his abstract paintings, the mother begins picking up young men, and the father staggers away, naked and howling into the wilderness. The young man's bisexuality is obviously used as a symbol. Though most critics reviewed the film favorably, there was only one point on which they all agreed: it was impossible to arrive at a definitive interpretation of the picture's theme. Pasolini's own vision of the young man is as follows:

> I leave it to the spectator–is the visitor God or is he the Devil? He is *not* Christ. The important thing is that he is sacred, a supernatural being. He is something from beyond . . . .

13. Face to Face

In *Face to Face* both plot and characters are the media through which Bergman's concerns with suicide, grief, and reality are explored. The story centers on Jenny (Liv Ullmann), a psychiatrist who tries to commit suicide; she is aided by the bisexual gynecologist Thomas (Erland Josephson). The film concentrates on Jenny's breakdown, her fears, her dreams. Thomas's role is the secondary one, but he is portrayed sympathetically if rather enigmatically. The ideas Bergman is dealing with are the immediacy of experience, the ease of getting hurt, and the enigmatic nature of suicide. Sexual orientations and emotional relationships are the vehicles for those ideas: Thomas is a man whose bisexuality is the bridge to his understanding and willing submersion in another's pain. He helps Jenny see that "love embraces everything–even death."

With *Gemini* and *The Shadow Box* the 1976-77 Broadway theater season illuminated bisexuality in a positive light after many years of either ignoring it or portraying the bisexual in a consistently negative light.

14. Gemini

This work by Albert Innaurato is a very funny play with a slight story line. Francis, a 21-year-old Ivy League student, has an affair with a female classmate but is also attracted sexually to her brother. Unexpectedly, the siblings visit him in his Philadelphia slum home. Jokes, pathos, and a larger-than-life picture follow. This entertaining play presents the bisexual positively. The feelings of the student are handled with delicacy. Francis's confusion and desires are viewed with warmth and sympathy, and the resolution of his sexual difficulties rings true. The play is not about bisexuality; that is not the issue. The play is about the goodness of people who are human enough to be warm and loving without shame.

15. The Shadow Box

The Shadow Box, by Michael Cristofer, won both the Tony Award and the Pulitzer Prize for the best play of 1976-77. The action occurs in a hospital where terminal cancer patients live out their last weeks or months in separate cottages with their loved ones. The play follows the plight of three dying people. One of them, Brian, is living in Cottage Two with his male lover. He is visited by his former wife. Brian, highly articulate and intelligent, knows that death is approaching quickly. His relationships with both the man and the woman in his life are touchingly portrayed. Once again the bisexual element is not the primary issue. As it is in *Gemini*, the bisexual "reality" is portrayed in a clear, sympathetic fashion permitting the bisexual's "truth"–both its good and bad points–to be shown.

THE "TRUTH"

1. Orlando

Virginia Woolf's story spans three centuries. The hero-heroine's biography begins with a boy of 16 at the close of Elizabeth the First's reign and ends with a woman of 35 listening to "the twelfth stroke of midnight, Thursday, the eleventh of October, Nineteen Hundred and Twenty-eight."

Both as a lusty, brawling young gentleman and later as a striking, modern young woman of impressive intelligence, Orlando sees monarchs come and go and fashions change through every age.

Unlike *Women in Love*, *Orlando* does not seek to impress on the reader the bisexual ideal. In its fanciful way, *Orlando* creates a character liberated from the restraints of gender identity in a way that allows us to see the possibility that gender itself is more fluid than we think. When still a man, Orlando finds his home in England uninhabitable because he is being pursued by a woman of frighteningly intense character. He asks King Charles to send him to Constantinople as Ambassador:

> The King was walking in Whitehall. Nell Gwyn was on his arm. She was pelting him with hazel nuts. 'Twas a thousand pities, that amorous lady sighed, that such a pair of legs should leave the country. Howbeit, the Fates were hard; she could do no more than toss one kiss over her shoulder before Orlando sailed.

Years later, as a woman on the deck of a ship returning to England, Orlando ponders the change in her condition. While wondering whether, if she leapt overboard, she could swim in the women's skirts she must now wear, she tosses her foot impatiently:

> . . . and showed an inch or two of calf. A sailor on the mast, who happened to look down at the moment, started so violently that he missed his footing and only saved himself by the skin of his teeth.

They are the same legs on the same human being. The responses of Nell Gwyn and the sailor are both sexual. But whereas Orlando the man can parade his shapely legs without a second thought, Orlando the woman must consider that if the sight of her ankles means the death of an honest fellow, she must in all humanity keep them covered and carry "the sacred responsibility of womanhood." The same legs on the same person gain acknowledgement from both sexes. Only when the leg belongs to the correct (opposite) sex is sexual desire permissible. The author's comment on the naturalness of bisexual response is obvious. But she is less interested in bisexuality per se than she is in the forces that cause men and women to play throughout a lifetime the gender role assigned by their genitals. On the continuum, Orlando is both man and woman in one person. As a woman she remembers her life as a man; that past is as much a part of her as her present. As she approaches England, she thinks of how she will never again be able to swear an oath in anger at anyone.

> . . . And I shall never be able to crack a man over the head, or tell him he lies in his teeth, or draw my sword and run him through the body, or sit among my peers, or wear a coronet, or walk in procession, or sentence a man to death, or lead an army, or prance down Whitehall on a charger, or wear seventy-two different medals on my breast. All I can do, once I set foot on English soil, is to pour out tea, and ask my lords how they like it. "D'you take sugar? D'you take cream?" And mincing out the words, she was horrified to perceive how low an opinion she was forming of the other sex, the manly, to which it had once been her pride to belong. "To fall from a mast-head," she thought, "because you see a woman's ankles; to dress up like a Guy Fawkes and parade the streets, so that women may praise you; to deny a woman teaching lest she may laugh at you; to be the slave of the frailest chit in petticoats, and yet to go about as if you were the Lords of creation.–Heavens!" she thought, "what fools they make of us– what fools we are!" And here it would seem from some ambiguity in her terms that she was censuring both sexes equally, as if she belonged to neither; and indeed, for the time being she seemed to vacillate; she was man; she was woman; she knew the secrets, shared the weaknesses of each.

Orlando knows the secrets and shares the weaknesses of both sexes. In a story less about the idea of gender and more about particular characters and events, Orlando might still have been *emotionally* intimate with both sexes, with or without being bisexual. But if in such a story the person who "knew the secrets" and "shared the weaknesses" of both genders *were* bisexual–and therefore "nonexistent" in society's prevailing view–the portrayal, while more "realistic," could never convey the transcendence of gender as convincingly as Woolf does in her fantasy.

Within this fantasy, the author asks us to understand her vision, her truth. When, as a young man, Orlando loved with all his heart and soul a beautiful Russian princess named Sasha, she broke his heart and darkened his soul. He was forced for the rest of his life–his *male* life– to ponder the meaning of love and even question its existence. Yet his love does not wane, even when he becomes a woman–quite the contrary; and much becomes clear:

> . . . though she herself was a woman, it was still a woman she loved; and if the consciousness of being of the same sex had any effect at all, it was to quicken and deepen those feelings which she had had as a man. For now a thousand hints and mysteries became plain to her that were then dark. Now, the obscurity, which divides the sexes and lets linger innumerable impurities in its gloom, was removed, and if there is anything in what the poet says about truth and beauty, this affection gained in beauty what it lost in falsity.

"Beauty." "Falsity." Isn't the larger portion of any civilized lifetime spent seeking beauty? Beauty to Virginia Woolf is understanding. This is not exactly a new idea. To know how another person feels is a part of wisdom, and in the eye of wisdom nothing is new; everything exists and always has existed. To Virginia Woolf, there is wisdom in the idea of bisexuality, of the androgynous human being comprising both male and female components.

2. The Left Hand of Darkness

An emissary by the name of Genly has been sent by a conglomerate of 80 worlds (the Union of Peoples) to the planet Winter to persuade the king of Karhide, a country of Winter, to join the conglomerate.

Winter is exactly what its name implies–a harsh, mostly frozen world where the people are in constant struggle with the elements. Although there are seasons, including summer, the winteriness is never completely gone. One gets the feeling that winter, after centuries, is bred into the marrow of its people and institutions.

Genly brings to the king an offer of trade, treaty, and alliance. Although he is self-described as black with a flat nose, Genly is a representation of the human male in general–black, white, red, or yellow–as we know him. What distinguishes him from the people of Winter, aside from the obvious differences of origin and culture, is his maleness. He is seen on Winter as a sexual freak because on Winter, men and women don't exist. The people of Winter are not male and female–nor are they neuter. They are potentials. Each person is a manwoman operating sexually in cycles of 26 to 28 days called kemmer.

> The culminant phase of kemmer lasts from two to five days, during which sexual drive and capacity are at maximum. It ends fairly abruptly, and if conception has not taken place, the individual returns to the somer phase within a few hours and the cycle begins anew. If the individual was in the female role and was impregnated, hormonal activity of course continues, and for the 8.4-month gestation period and the 6- to 8-month lactation period this individual remains female. The male sexual organs remain retracted (as they are in somer), the breasts enlarge somewhat, and the pelvic girdle widens. With the cessation of lactation the female re-enters somer and becomes once more a perfect androgyne.

The people of Winter are not "bisexual," in that they are not men, not women. But the bisexual idea underlies Ursula K. Le-Guin's *The Left Hand of Darkness:*

> . . . Anyone can turn his hand to anything. This sounds very simple, but its psychological effects are incalculable. The fact that everyone between seventeen and thirty-five or so is liable to be . . . "tied down to childbearing," implies that no one is quite so thoroughly "tied down" here as women, elsewhere, are likely to be–psychologically or physically. Burden and privilege are shared out pretty equally; everybody has the same risk to run or choice to make. Therefore nobody here is quite so free as a free male anywhere else.
> . . . A child has no psycho-sexual relationship to his mother and father. There is no myth of Oedipus on Winter.
> . . . There is no unconsenting sex, no rape. As with most mammals other than man, coitus can be performed only by mutual invitation and consent; otherwise it is not possible.

Seduction certainly is possible, but it must have to be awfully well timed.

    . . . There is no division of humanity into strong and weak halves, protective/protected, dominant/submissive, owner/ chattel, active/passive. In fact the whole tendency to dualism that pervades human thinking may be found to be lessened, or changed, on Winter.

APPENDIX B
Bisexual Survey Results

The questionnaire was given to the first 150 people coming to the Bisexual Forum in New York City during 1976-77. Six declined to participate. Of those who did, 16 (10 men and 6 women) were heterosexual, and 1 man was homosexual; 127 were bisexual through self-identification, bisexual experiences, or both.

Following are the results of the survey: *

1. Sex: N = 144   Males = 103   Females = 41

2. Age:

Females: N = 36   Males: N = 99
           N.A. = 5   N.A. = 4
           Aver. = 28.5 years   Aver. = 32.4 years

---

*The following abbreviations are used here:

N = number	Homo. = homosexual	Aver. = average
N.A. = no answer	Bi. = bisexual	
N.D. = never did	Sep. = separated	
Het. = heterosexual	Div. = divorced	

3. Education:

Males: N = 96   Females: N = 35
            N.A. = 7   N.A. = 6
            Aver. = 16.1 years   Aver. = 15 years

4. Which parent were you closer to:

Bi. Females: Mother = 13   37%
N = 35   Father = 13   37%
                Both = 6   17%
                N.A. = 3   9%

Bi. Males: Mother = 64   69%
N = 92   Father = 6   7%
                Both = 19   21%
                N.A. = 3   3%

5. Marital Status:

Males: N = 103   Females: N = 41
Never married = 59   58%   Never married = 23   56%
     Married   = 20   19%   Married   =   6   15%
Sep. or Div.   = 24   23%   Sep. or Div.   = 10   24%
       N.A.   =   0   N.A.   =   2   5%

Males & Females: Never married = 82   57%
N = 144   Married   = 26   18%
                    Sep. or Div.   = 34   24%
                           N.A.   =   2   1%

6. Current Living Arrangements:

	Males	%	Females	%	Both	%
Alone	54	51	14	34	68	46
Spouse	16	15	5	12	21	14
Friend/Lover	11	10	4	10	15	10
Parent(s)	8	8	6	15	14	10
Roommate	7	7	6	15	13	9
Child(ren)	2	2	5	12	7	5
Relative	4	4	1	2	5	3
School	1	1	0	0	1	1
N.A.	3	3	0	0	3	2
Total	106*		41*		147*	

* Some respondents gave more than one answer.

7. Do you think of yourself as:

__ 0. Exclusively heterosexual
__ 1. Predominantly heterosexual, only insignificantly homosexual
__ 2. Predominantly heterosexual, but significantly homosexual
__ 3. Equally heterosexual and homosexual
__ 4. Predominantly homosexual, but significantly heterosexual
__ 5. Predominantly homosexual, only insignificantly heterosexual
__ 6. Exclusively homosexual

	Female	*Male*	*Both*	%
0	6	11	17	12
1	14	26	40	28
2	5	20	25	17
3	7	19	26	18
4	4	10	14	10
5	2	11	13	9
6	1	1	2	1
N.A.	2	5	7	5
Total	41	103	144	

Of those that answered 1-5, the average was for females = 2.4 and males = 2.5

8. In the past *month,* indicate the number and gender of people with whom you had sex:

Bi. Males:	*Females*	*Males*
	N = 89	N = 86
	N.A. = 3	N.A. = 6
	Aver. = 1.7	Aver. = 2.4
	(None = 30)	(None = 27)
Bi. Females:	N = 30	N = 32
	N.A. = 5	N.A. = 3
	Aver. = 0.7	Aver. = 1.5
	(None = 17)	(None = 9)

9. In the past *year,* indicate the number and gender of people with whom you had sex:

Bi. Males:	*Females*	*Males*
	N = 86	N = 82
	N.A. = 6	N.A. = 10
	Aver. = 9.2	Aver. = 12.9
	(None = 11)	(None = 8)
Bi. Females:	N = 28	N = 30
	N.A. = 8	N.A. = 5
	Aver. = 3.0	Aver. = 4.7
	(None = 6)	(None = 1)

10. Considering only your close friends whose sexual orientation you know, what percent are:

Bi. Females:		
	N = 30	Het. = 74.2%
	N.A. = 5	Homo. = 18.0%
		Bi. = 7.8%
Bi. Males:		
	N = 86	Het. = 69.6%
	N.A. = 6	Homo. = 20.2%
		Bi. = 10.2%
Total Bis.:		
	N = 116	Het. = 70.8%
	N.A. = 11	Homo. = 19.6%
		Bi. = 9.6%

11A. Do you consider yourself bisexual?

Bisexuals:*	*Male*	*Female*	*Both*	
Yes	71	27	98	77%
No	10	5	15	12%
?	7	2	9	7%
N.A.	4	1	5	4%

*Included here were respondents who had bisexual experience, even though they did not identify themselves as bisexual.

11B. If so, at what age did you first consider yourself bisexual?

Bi. Males: 24.1 yrs. (aver.) *Bi. Females:* 24.4 yrs. (aver.)
N = 63 N = 23
Total Bis.: 24.2 years aver. N = 86

12. How old were you when you first realized that you had sexual feelings toward:

Females: age __ N.D. __ Males: age __ N.D. __
Bi. Males:

Females	*Males*
N = 82	N = 78
N.D. = 0	N.D. = 4
N.A. = 10	N.A. = 10
Aver. = 13.1 years	Aver. = 16.0 years

Bi. Females:

N = 31	N = 27
N.D. = 1	N.D. = 0
N.A. = 3	N.A. = 8
Aver. = 17 years	Aver: = 11.3 years

13. How old were you when you had your first sexual experience with a *female*?

Bi. Females	*Bi. Males*
N = 30	N = 88
N.D. = 4	N.D. = 1
N.A. = 1	N.A. = 3
Aver. = 23 years	Aver. = 16 years

14. How old were you when you had your first sexual experience with a *male*?

Bi. Females	Bi. Males
N = 35	N = 84
N.D. = 0	N.D. = 3
N.A. = 0	N.A. = 5
Aver. = 15.5 years	Aver. = 17.8 years

13. vs. 14. Comparing those respondents who had their first sexual experience with a female as compared to a male, we find that for:

Bi. Females:	1st experience with a female	=	6	17%
	1st experience with a male	=	24	69%
	age of 1st experience was equal	=	0	
	N.A.	=	5	14%
Bi. Males:	1st experience with a female	=	43	47%
	1st experience with a male	=	33	36%
	age of 1st experience was equal	=	6	6%
	N.A.	=	10	11%

15. At what age did you first experience penile-vaginal intercourse?

Bi. Males	Bi. Females
N = 83	N = 34
N.D. = 3	N.D. = 1
N.A. = 6	N.A. = 0
Aver. = 17.6 years	Aver. = 18.1 years

16. In the past year, how or where have you found *female* sex partners? and

17. In the past year, how or where have you found *male* sex partners?

Bi. Females: N = 35	*Female Partners*	*Male Partners*
Friends	13	10
Parties	3	3
Rap, disc. grps.	3	2
Bars	4	3
School	2	3
Knew from before	–	2
Public pickup	–	3
Work	1	3
Soc. groups, clubs	1	5
Husband	–	1
Bi. groups	2	1
Gay groups	3	–
Swinging, group sex	3	1
Everywhere	–	3
Misc.	2	5
None, didn't	5	2
N.A.	7	6
Total	49*	53*

*Some respondents gave more than one answer.

Bi. Males: N = 92	Female Partners	Male Partners
Friends	18	15
Parties	9	8
Rap, disc. grps.	4	–
Bars	7	24
Baths	–	12
Movies	–	4
Public pickup	7	18
Work	10	3
School	6	2
Knew from before	9	4
Wife	5	–
Prostitution	3	–
Disco & dances	6	1
Soc. grps. & clubs	4	–
Gay & bi. org.	–	3
Ads	1	1
Everywhere	9	3
Misc.	13	7
None, didn't	6	24
N.A.	17	12
Total	134*	141*

*Some respondents gave more than one answer.

18. Do you prefer sex with:

__ Males __ Females __ Males and females equally

Bi. Males N = 92		Bi. Females N = 35	
Males = 19	20%	Males = 11	31%
Females = 32	35%	Females = 7	20%
Both equal = 32	35%	Both equal = 14	40%
N.A. = 9	10%	N.A. = 3	9%

19. Have you been involved in sexual activity with two or more other people at the same time:
In the past month __ Past year __ Your whole life __

	Last Month		*Last Year*		*Whole Life*	
Bi. Males:						
N = 92						
Yes	24	26%	44	48%	57	62%
No	53	58%	31	34%	15	16%
N.A.	15	16%	17	18%	20	22%
Bi. Females:						
N = 35						
Yes	5	14%	14	40%	23	66%
No	27	77%	17	49%	9	26%
N.A.	3	9%	4	11%	3	8%
Total Bis.:						
N = 127						
Yes	29	22.8%	58	45.7%	80	63.0%
No	80	63.0%	48	37.8%	24	18.9%
N.A.	18	14.2%	21	16.5%	23	18.1%

20. In your sexual fantasies, do you imagine having sex with:
__ Females mostly __ Males mostly __ Sometimes female, sometimes male

Bi. Females:		*Bi. Males*	
N = 38		N = 92	
Fem. = 7	20.0%	Fem. = 19	20.7%
Male = 9	25.7%	Male = 28	30.4%
Both = 13	37.2%	Both = 45	48.9%
N.A. = 6	17.1%	N.A. = 0	

21. If you could begin life anew, would you rather be:

__ Heterosexual __ Homosexual __ Bisexual

Bi. Males:		*Bi. Females:*		*Total Bis.:*	
N = 92		N = 35		N = 127	
Het. = 21	22.8%	Het. = 4	11.4%	Het. = 25	19.7%
Homo. = 2	2.2%	Homo. = 2	5.7%	Homo. = 4	3.2%
Bi. = 60	65.2%	Bi. = 26	74.3%	Bi. = 86	67.7%
N.A. = 9	9.8%	N.A. = 3	8.6%	N.A. = 12	9.4%

22. Have you ever sought counseling for problems relating to your sexual orientation:

Bi. Males:		*Bi. Females:*		*Total Bis.:*	
N = 92		N = 35		N = 127	
Yes = 35	38%	Yes = 9	25.7%	Yes = 44	34.6%
No = 52	56.5%	No = 21	60%	No = 73	57.5%
N.A. = 5	5.5%	N.A. = 5	14.3%	N.A. = 10	7.9%

21. vs. 22.

Of the 86 bisexuals who answered they would rather be bisexual if they could begin life anew:

  24 (27.9%) did seek counseling
  57 (66.3%) did not seek counseling
   5 (5.8%) did not answer question 22

Of the 41 bisexuals who would in a new life rather be heterosexual, homosexual, or did not answer the question:

  20 (48.8%) did seek counseling
  16 (39%) did not seek counseling
   5 (12.2%) did not answer question 22

23. Who of the following know that you are bisexual:

	Bi. Males N = 92	Bi. Females N = 35	Total Bis. N = 127	
Parent(s)				
Yes	10	3	13	10.2%
No	52	15	67	52.8%
N.A.	30	17	47	37.0%
Sibling(s)				
Yes	8	2	10	7.9%
No	55	16	71	55.9%
N.A.	29	17	46	36.2%
Spouse				
Yes	13	6	19	15.0%
No	47	11	58	45.6%
N.A.	32	18	50	39.4%
Relative(s)				
Yes	9	3	12	9.4%
No	53	15	68	53.6%
N.A.	30	17	47	37.0%
Work Assoc.				
Yes	15	10	25	19.7%
No	48	9	57	44.9%
N.A.	29	16	45	35.4%
Friends				
Yes	57	22	79	62.2%
No	11	–	11	8.7%
N.A.	24	13	37	29.1%

For the answers to the following five questions, see Chapter 8, page 107.

24. What are the main pleasures or advantages of being bisexual?

25. What are the main problems or disadvantages of being bisexual?

26. Do you take pride in being bisexual? Explain briefly.

27. Do you have feelings of shame or guilt in being bisexual?

28. What are your feelings on your own bisexuality and bisexuality in general?

Bibliography

Baldwin, James. *Giovanni's Room*. New York: Dell Publishing Co., 1964.

Bell, Clive. *Civilization*. New York: Harcourt Brace and Co., 1926.

Bieber, I., H. J. Dain, P. R. Dince, M. G. Drelich, H. G. Grand, R. H. Gundlach, M. W. Kremer, A. H. Rifkin, C. B. Wilber, and T. B. Bieber, (1962). *Homosexuality: A Psychoanalytic Study*. New York: Basic Books.

Billy, John O. G., Koray Tanfer, William R. Grady, and Daniel H. Klepinger, "The Sexual Behavior of Men in the United States." *Family Planning Perspectives*. Vol. 25, No. 2 (March/April 1993), pp. 52-60.

Blumstein, Philip W., and Pepper Schwartz. "Bisexuality in Men." *Urban Life*, Vol. 5, No. 3 (Oct. 1976), pp. 339-358.

_____. "Bisexuality in Women." *Archives of Sexual Behavior*, Vol. 5 (March 1976), pp. 171-181.

Bode, Janet. *View from Another Closet*. New York: Hawthorn Books, 1976.

Bolton, Mary, and Peter Weatherburn. *Literature Review on Bisexuality and HIV Transmission*. Report Commissioned by the Global Programme on AIDS, World Health Organization, Academic Dept. of Public Health, St. Mary's Hospital Medical School. London: 1990.

Brain, Robert. *Friends and Lovers*. New York: Basic Books, 1976.

Brown, Howard. *Familiar Faces, Hidden Lives: The Story of Homosexual Men in America Today*. New York: Harcourt Brace Jovanovich, 1976.

Buxton, Amity Pierce. *The Other Side of the Closet*. Santa Monica, CA: IBS Press, Inc., 1991.

Colette. *Earthly Paradise*. New York: Farrar, Straus & Giroux, 1966.

Crosland, Margaret. *Colette, The Difficulty of Loving*. New York: Bobbs Merrill, 1973.

Dannecker, Martin, and Reimut Reiche. *Der Gewöhnliche Homosexuelle*. Frankfurt: S. Fischer Verlag GmbH, 1974.

David, Deborah S., and Robert Brannon. *The Forty-Nine Percent Majority: The Male Sex Role*. Reading, MA: Addison-Wesley, 1976.

Drury, Allen. *Advise and Consent*. New York: Avon Books, 1974.

Fox, Ronald C. *Coming Out Bisexual: Identity, Behavior, and Sexual Orientation Self-Disclosure*. Unpublished doctoral dissertation, California Institute of Integral Studies, San Francisco, CA, 1993.

Freedman, Alfred M., and Harold I. Kaplan, Eds. *Comprehensive Textbook of Psychiatry*. Baltimore: Williams and Wilkins, 1967.

Freud, Sigmund. 1925, *SE*, XIX, p. 258.

Geller, Thomas. *Bisexuality: A Reader and Sourcebook*. California: Times Change Press, 1990.

Gilliatt, Penelope. *Sunday Bloody Sunday*. New York: Viking Press, 1971.

Goode, Eriche, and Richard Troiden. *Sexual Deviance and Sexual Deviants*. New York: William Morrow and Co., 1975.

Gould, Robert E. "Homosexuality." *The New York Times Magazine*, February 24, 1974.

Harrison, James. "A Critical Evaluation of Research on 'Masculinity/Femininity.'" Department of Psychology Dissertation, New York University, 1975.

Hatterer, Lawrence J. *Changing Homosexuality in the Male*. New York: McGraw-Hill, 1970.

Heilbrun, Carolyn G. *Toward a Recognition of Androgyny*. New York: Knopf, 1973.

Hemingway, Ernest. "The Sea Change" in *The Short Stories of Ernest Hemingway*. New York: Charles Scribner's Sons, 1921-38.

Holroyd, Michael. *Lytton Strachey*. New York: Holt, Rinehart and Winston, 1967.

Horney, Karen. *Neurosis and Human Growth*. New York: W. W. Norton, 1950.

Hunt, Morton. *Sexual Behavior in the Seventies*. Chicago: Playboy Press, 1974.

Hutchins, Loraine and Lani Kaahumanu, Eds. *Bi Any Other Name:*

Bisexual People Speak Out. Boston: Alyson Publications, Inc., 1991.

Hyde, H. Montgomery. *Oscar Wilde: A Biography.* New York: Farrar, Straus and Giroux, 1975.

Johnstone, J. K. *The Bloomsbury Group.* New York: Noonday Press, 1963.

Kardiner, A., A. Karush, and L. Ovesey, (1959). "A Methodological Study of Freudian Theory." *Journal of Nervous and Mental Diseases*, Vol. 129, pp. 133-143.

Karlen, Arno. *Sexuality & Homosexuality.* New York: W. W. Norton, 1971.

Katz, Jonathan. *Gay American History.* New York: Thomas Y. Crowell Co., 1976.

Kinsey, Alfred C., Wardell B. Pomeroy, and Clyde E. Martin. *Sexual Behavior in the Human Male.* Philadelphia, W. B. Saunders Co., 1948.

Kinsey, Alfred C., Wardell B. Pomeroy, Clyde E. Martin, and Paul H. Gebhard. *Sexual Behavior in the Human Female.* Philadelphia: W. B. Saunders Co., 1953.

Klein, Fritz, B. Sepekoff, and T. J. Wolf. "Sexual Orientation: A Multivariable Dynamic Process" in Klein, F., and T. J. Wolf, Eds. *Bisexualities: Theory and Research.* New York: The Haworth Press, 1985.

Klein, Fritz. "The Need to View Sexual Orientation as a Multivariable Dynamic Process: A Theoretical Perspective" in McWhirter, D. P., S. A. Sanders, J. M. Reinisch, *Homosexuality/Heterosexuality.* New York, Oxford: Oxford University Press, 1990.

Koestler, Arthur. *The Act of Creation.* New York: Macmillan, 1964.

Lawrence, D. H. *The Fox.* New York: Viking Press, 1923.

————. *Women in Love.* New York: Viking Press, 1920.

LeGuin, Ursula K. *The Left Hand of Darkness.* New York: Ace Books, 1969.

Levin, Robert J., and Amy Levin: "Sexual Pleasure." *Redbook*, Vol. 145, No. 5 and 6, September and October 1975.

Licht, Hans. *Sexual Life in Ancient Greece.* London: The Abbey Library, 1932.

Mann, Thomas. *Death in Venice.* New York: Knopf, 1930.

Maugham, Robin. *Escape from the Shadows.* New York: McGraw-Hill, 1972.

McWhirter, David, and Andrew Mattison. Personal Communication, 1977.

Mead, Margaret. "Bisexuality: What's It All About?" *Redbook*, January 1975.

Menard, W. *The Two Worlds of Somerset Maugham.* Los Angeles: Sherbourne Press, 1965.

Mitchell, Yvonne. *Colette: A Taste for Life.* New York: Harcourt, Brace, Jovanovich, 1975.

Money, John. quoted in "The New Bisexuals." *Time*, May 13, 1974.

Money, John, and Anke A. Ehrhardt. *Man and Woman, Boy and Girl.* Baltimore: The Johns Hopkins University Press, 1972.

Morris, Desmond. *Intimate Behaviour.* New York: Random House, 1972.

Mullahy, Patrick. *Oedipus Myth and Complex.* New York: Grove Press, 1948.

Murray, Jane. *The Kings & Queens of England.* New York: Charles Scribner's Sons, 1974.

Nicolson, Nigel. *Portrait of a Marriage.* New York: Atheneum, 1973.

Off Pink Collective, Eds. *Bisexual Lives.* London: Off Pink Publishing, 1988.

Painter, G. D. *André Gide: A Critical & Biographical Study.* London: Arthur Barker, 1951.

Reinhardt, Regina Ursula. *Bisexual Women in Heterosexual Relationships.* Dissertation published in: Research Abstracts International, Fall 1986, Vol. II, Issue 3, p. 67.

Renault, Mary. *The Nature of Alexander.* New York: Pantheon Books, 1975.

Rosenbaum, S. P., Ed. *The Bloomsbury Group.* Toronto: University of Toronto Press, 1975.

Rowse, A. L. *Homosexuals in History.* New York: Macmillan, 1977.

Ruitenbeek, Hendrik. *The New Sexuality.* New York: New Viewpoints, 1974.

Rule, Jane. *Lesbian Images.* New York: Doubleday, 1975.

Saghir, Marcel T., and Eli Robins. *Male and Female Homosexuality*. Baltimore: Williams and Wilkins, 1973.

Shainess, Natalie. quoted in "The New Bisexuals." *Time*, May 13, 1974.

Sievers, W. David. *Freud on Broadway*. New York: Cooper Square Publishers, 1970.

Singer, June. *Androgyny*. New York: Anchor Press, 1976.

Socarides, Charles W. *The Overt Homosexual*. New York: Grune and Stratton, 1968.

_____. "Bisexual Chic: Anyone Goes." *Newsweek*, May 27, 1974.

Stekel, Wilhelm. *Bi-Sexual Love*. New York: Emerson Books, 1950 (1922).

Tavris, Carol. "Men & Women Report Their Views on Masculinity." *Psychology Today*, January 1977.

Tielman, Rob A.P., Manuel Carballo, and Aart C. Hendriks, Eds. *Bisexuality and HIV/AIDS: A Global Perspective*. Buffalo, New York: Prometheus Books, 1991.

Vidal, Gore. *The City and the Pillar*. New York: New American Library, 1974.

Warren, Patricia Nell. *The Front Runner*. New York: William Morrow and Co., 1974.

Watzlawick, Paul, J. H. Beavin, and D. D. Jackson. *Pragmatics of Human Communication*. New York: W. W. Norton, 1967.

Weinberg, George. *Society and the Healthy Homosexual*. New York: St. Martin's Press, 1972.

Weinberg, Martin S., and Colin J. Williams. *Male Homosexuals*. New York: Oxford University Press, 1974.

Weinberg, Martin S., Colin J. Williams and Douglas Pryor, *Dual Attraction: Bisexuality in the Age of AIDS*. New York: Oxford University Press, 1994.

Weinrich, James D. *Sexual Landscapes*. New York: Charles Scribner's Sons, 1987.

Weise, Elizabeth Reba, Ed. *Closer to Home, Bisexuality and Feminism*. Seattle: The Seal Press, 1992.

Williams, Tennessee. *Memoirs*. New York: Doubleday, 1972.

Wolf, Charlotte. *Bisexuality: A Study*. London: Quartet Books Ltd., 1977.

Woolf, Virginia. *Orlando*. New York: Harcourt Brace Jovanovich, 1928.

_____ . *The Death of the Moth*. New York: Harcourt Brace and Co., 1942.

Zessen, van G. J. and T. Sandfort (editors). *Sexualiteit in Nederland*. Lisse, Swets, en Zeitlinger, 1991.

Index